IN SERIES

THE SYNTHESIS
IN SERIES

in here was previously published as a chapbook by Monkey Puzzle Press in 2013; "Lines of Bisection" originally appeared in *Whole Beast Rag*; "Me Too" originally appeared in *Frag Lit*.

IN HERE

I advance pointing to my mask.
—Barthes

CONTENTS

READER'S NOTE

There is memoir.
There is not-memoir.
There are both memoir and not-memoir.
There is neither memoir nor not-memoir.

AGAINST THE NEBULOUS BORDERLINE

In the field of my reflection I can never meet with anything but the consciousness which is mine. But the Other is the indispensable mediator between myself and me.
                                        —Sartre

Two eyes. One I. No self.
Two eyes staring out from the void.
A world of facts.
I see everything. Except mirrors, which are holes I disappear in.

I fall through.

I tumble down, caroming against language and thought and history. This must be the birth canal of consciousness of consciousness.

If nothing is a nothing and has no boundary, how is there an outside of nothing, a beyond in being, that is a something? If there is something, where is there left for nothing to be? And if there is no nothing, what does something mean? What did it mean before I was born, before I fell through the mirror?

Either some*thing* and no*thing* are two sides of the same *thing* or what good are these words?

What are the alternatives?

Alternatives to what?

I'm standing on air
Or perhaps I'm still falling
And this is the view from the descent.

The problem of subjectivity is not to solve the causal mystery; the problem of subjectivity is subjectivity causes the problem.

* * *

In the middle, the center, I am invisible. I look out. I take in. To the left is Sandy, to the right is Flor, to their either sides are Bridget and Victoria. There's Isaac down there. And Zoe. These are people. They exist.

Even with glasses I squint to distinguish persons, but I'm pretty sure they're there and if I reached out I could touch them. There is optimism. I stare straight ahead encountering these rewards.

Earlier, I drank two beers. Two beers is a good number of beers to drink. The experience of being me is pleasant right now.

I await my entertainment.

It occurs to me that I drank whiskey, too, and thought of Dylan.

There are words, words, words, all these words, sounds but no voices, utterances without meaning. I skip ahead.

Now there are two men on stage. This is a performance. These men are black. One has light skin, one has dark skin, but both identify as black. The men are talking about, among other things, being black. Conversation goes like this:

Q—
Q—
Q—
A—
Q—
Q—
Q—
A—

A. being pursued by Q., whose assignment seems to be cornering A. long enough that he can get his hands on him and make him hold still. A. will not be held onto, resists the boundaries, is elusive. Q. is nervous, wants A. to like him, was set up. Here I am, entertained.

Dylan comes to mind again: "I got nothing to say about these things I write. I mean, I just write 'em. I don't have to say anything about 'em. I don't write 'em for any reason. There's no great message." A. writes books and says when they're out of his hands they're in yours.

If I reached out to touch him my hands would plunge right through. My hands
are . . . my hands are . . . nimble? I want to . . . I want to . . . touch?

Don't look back. I mean it. *Dont Look Back.*

A. says, "I'm not black when I wake up. I'm just I. It's not until someone calls
me black that I become black to myself."

Don't look back. Please, don't look back, please.

A. says, "It's the same for anyone. You start the day just minding your business,
looking out. It's not until someone catches you that you become self-conscious."

* * *

The self only comes into existence at the point of conflict with not-self, but how
can a thing that doesn't yet exist rub up against something that does?

I'm in here meaning this room meaning this body meaning alongside you and in
front of you but either way with you.

And I can move these hands. I swear, I can move them.

I'm moving them for you.

LINES OF BISECTION
AN (A)E(S)TH(ET)IC(AL) SUSPENSION OF THE TELELOGICAL

There is no human who exists metaphysically.
—Kierkegaard

From wherever I begin, from there I set out with a destination in mind (even when the destination is the process), an endpoint envisioned (even when the envisioning is of an endpoint that will present itself at some undisclosed point in time to some as yet undisclosed—or unconceived—future self), or imagined, or invented *post hoc*—a step having been already taken from the origin—all of these are endings. The forward thrust of the moving edge of my consciousness traces a line leading into an infinitesimal unknown, the receding limit of destiny on the horizon. What vague outline beckons? Cohesion, completion, consciousness finally circled and contented (a self in full). The teleological pull of a promise whose appeal is so appealing for the sake of the unkeptness it promises (falsely) to relieve.

A writer who sets himself a problem has already set his answer too: this arrangement of words follows that.

Fig. 1. Lines of Bisection

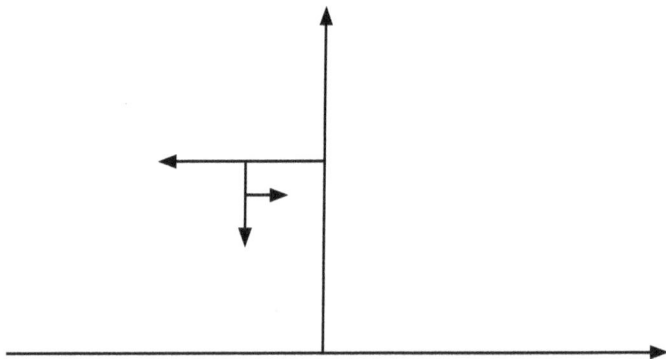

Here is *my* problem: here is the goal I never obtain: *there* is the moving target of my self-satisfaction, my self-acceptance, my self-identify, my self itself: all things gathered up under the covered structure of this sturdy timeline: thoughts occurring *in order*: this idea always needing and invoking the next: no periodicity in this chain, just links of instances soldered at their endpoints and melding into the causal chain of the history of this sentence: it reaches where it needs to reach and no further: it reaches out to the responsibility to elucidate:

My life made sense when I was a physics student: the teacher said Tycho Brahe had a wooden nose and a weak bladder—I too was ready to represent science and the certain knowledge of precisely (if my results were empirically falsifiable, they were still consistent(ly bold)) where the shoe would hit the floor: my vector was magnanimous and I could identify crystal forms in Europan water without a telescope: I invented the future every time I looked at the sky. This period of my life, though, was over before it reached its midpoint: I learned of Zeno of Elea and lost all sense of progress: I was past Newton and bound for Feynman when the conservation of linear momentum was disproved by the gravitational force of my human fucking heart (q.e.d.) . . .

I got to Feynman anyway because anyone who writes like he bongos is worth the rhythm of a dance through possibility where probability leads to the necessity of answering the paradox in whatever terms are available to you: these are my terms: existence and essence, in that order: everything is up for grabs and the narrative resists, resists conclusion . . . where would it end?

But the synthetic urge was strong in me and I blew through the idea that I didn't write this whole thing, this whole endless stream of thing leading on to thing, for the sake of a metaphysics that would make Hegel jealous (if only he'd been born later, if only . . .) . . . process me processing my process as I tie strings across valleys and tell Nietzsche to walk:

That's where I'm suspended, alone with everyone else: halfway between always and the philosopher of the future (you've heard the future comes the day after tomorrow): be ready: to jump: our souls spread wide as we reach for the summation that will give us a moment to breathe if it gives us anything at all—and if it gives us nothing, nothing we will take: we are strong. And we make declarations.

* * *

That's the history, summarily told: physics and philosophy written, only silence left untranslated—and I fear I'll never arrive.

Moving forward, the question is this: the situation is this:

Looking back, I see the journey started long ago and the terminus is no closer, though much ground has been gained. I proceed.

I always proceed.

The project is clear: to write the self into being, to compose a life.

But the rules keep changing, my keyboard keys keep sticking: only the metaphysical buttons are working and I can't push them anymore. I can't do it. They won't go.

The question remains: which self I will create (which one created I?) and which one is doing the writing and how are they related? And the answer hasn't changed in a million evolutionary years: I'm barefoot here and there's no ground beneath my feet.

I ripped the bootstraps clean off my boots.

The story keeps restarting; I keep restarting it, waiting for the true, the definitive, to present itself. I don't believe in anything, but it's in my faithful bones to try.

Time and words and self all tumbling around and spiraling in on one another . . . the noise amplifying and magnifying and crescendoing and et cetera and ending in:

THE PROBLEM OF TWO

Je est un autre
—Rimbaud

There is another other
in the other of every

Another
—Ed Bok Lee

i want to write a memoir of another other: another's other

i want to advance certain theories of uncertainty
i want to advance them where they don't belong
   and let them live

i want to tell someone else's lies for awhile, save us both some trouble

i want not to be asked who this is for (this is for you)
i want not to be asked if this is true (this is true)

i want to say that life and words are mine and yours
i want to rhyme *Tuesday* with *eternity*
   and gather sustenance from my own schemes
i want you to read about when I killed S.
   and recognize you killed him too

i want you to know all suicides are failures, even the successes:
they're pragmatic in the worst way:
effective but not efficient
and sure not elegant

* * *

in the beginning (there was a beginning)
(not to mention a beginning to be a beginning)
there was nowhere to stand
in a breath there was sound
and from sound came space
and from space came fear

and do you see now what *inelegant* means?

from one springs one
from two spring many—

we are alone only because there are so many of us

* * *

I killed S. because it was either him or me.

Let me explain.

Allergic to my mother's milk, I produced my own nectar. I sated myself on the wind that I named my god and became powerful. I dug roots and picked berries out of paradise. I drank it down raw, killed with my bare hands, and then breathed the life back into my victims. I was an animator.

Men trembled at the smell of me—I stank of sweat and wildness.

And while I was their hero, I was my own hero as well.

* * *

It's insidious how these things begin.

My garden was bountiful.

I was a sprawling giant in a shrinking world, and—oh, you already know, I got squeezed. My father called me son and his name was my name. It's an old story, but it was new to me:

S., the *deus ex machina* of this story, knew how to compromise and survive and make do with what he got (and didn't mind not getting what was his due). Those years were necessary years, but the things that rescue us eventually come to bind us down; we must return double the great harms that are done to us or we will rot. I killed him, he didn't die, I killed him again, and again I will kill him again and again. And father—his name is my name—I killed him too. The killing never ceases.

* * *

I found a journal and I wrote the word. I filled it all up with words. And when I ran out of page, I turned to another. Another and another. Soon—years, but soon—there was a stack of these tomes. My most valued possessions, these books were the record of my becoming. The self appeared finally there, the present narrated into existence from the present through the past, the past that I wrote, the past I created, the past I made mine. I owned it all and I was coherent and it was real and I was full again. *I* was viable. The conclusion, the time sensitive *I* of that moment, was accounted for. I named myself, memoired the story that was needed.

And the end of the story is this:

I waited for a night when I was alone at home and opened a bottle of blood-heavy red wine and sat by the fire to read. I read through these years of journals, these pages of my history, these marks of my being. I read them page by page, and after each page there was a great ripping before I dropped each leaf slowly onto the hot red embers below, where they burned in turn and became the stuff I breathe.

FACTS

I am responsible. I didn't not ask for this, but I am responsible. I am responsible for me and I am responsible for you. I am weak and I am flawed and I will fail you. I accept this and for this too I take responsibility. This is not an apology. When the time comes, if it is necessary, I will defeat you. My strength is large. ██ I am lucky for my vigor and luckier for my vulnerability. Roger Federer's forehand makes Platonists of the illiterate and corrects my most hopeless hours. The smell of McDonald's still makes me wish I was still six years old. When the apocalypse comes you will find me at McDonald's—but not a moment sooner. I have cursed myself silly after nights of drinking, pausing only to throw up in all the wrong places and lose even the strength to hate. I will self-destruct and it will not matter; I will survive every eruption. These are facts. I write them because they are true. There is more: I have masturbated while driving, but might not have thought to do so had a friend not recommended it for long solitary journeys. I come up with stuff, I'm creative in a way, but I need a spark. These facts all occur in very specific contexts, all context being very specific. I have committed crimes. I have hurt people. I am helpless in the face of beauty. ██████████████████████████████████ My knee hurts. I have read everything David Foster Wallace has written and might do it again. Ditto Chaung Tzu. And others. I fear I will never find time for Heidegger. Or Faulkner. I can't say why them. A friend tells me "that's fine, there are plenty of dead white guys." If my knee doesn't get better soon, I may start drinking more. I am infatuated with Zadie Smith's mind—or at least I appreciate the way she arranges words on pages. If you upset my little sister she will stomp you. She is small, but she is ferocious. I told my students I would bring them a happy story to read next class. Next class I told them I didn't know any. This was not totally true. I enjoy using drugs, especially psilocybin. Cocaine was never really my thing. Plain old caffeine and alcohol are where it's at for me now. I would take up smoking if I had more courage. Or if I had less. The tiger is a magnificent creature. I will be sad if we extinct them, and I will be sad if we don't. I will be sad. I don't trust people who are not occasionally sad. I have doubts. I wonder sometimes if I love running as much as I say I do. And then I go for a run and realize that was a stupid question. I'm happy. This should be making sense by now. I am not as smart or as conscious as I want to be. I am human. I love easily. I know deep inside of me both meanings of pride. Today is Tuesday. Tomorrow is an eternity. The philosopher is not coming. Prepare yourselves. If I die in the forest I will be the lucky one. You are not safe. Wherever you are right now reading this, you are not safe. Danger is out there, stalking you. It will come for you. My advice is this: Do not be afraid. Be Mindful. Go out from there. Go out. It is better to be changed by acid than to be changed by money. Aristotle is still underrated as a moral philosopher. Black Friday is not a holiday. Yes, not acquiescence, is a compliment. When you love someone you answer yes before the question gets asked. There is no martyrdom in love. These are gifts. You give what you can. One barrel of oil is equivalent to twenty-five years of human labor. Years. The fact is we need to think about that. Then sharpen knives and put down cola. This is real. All of it. I wrote Michael Dukakis a letter in 1988 saying, my god, man, do something. One of his volunteers thanked me for my support. The next month I got kicked out of second grade. I was class president. What choice was there? I know the cost of everything I've lost. I learned calculus sitting in the hallway waiting for my time to come, wondering if it had already gone. I am angry. I demand changes. There are things I never should have done. I did them anyway, knowing full well. There are people I should apologize to but don't. There are people who should apologize to me—I hope they never do. There are worse things in life than failure. Michael Jordan could never be the next Michael Jordan. Following Penny Hardaway's career arc, I learned of adult disappointment and the anguish of potential. If you think it doesn't all come back to basketball, you're wrong. It does. For five years, watching Steve Nash and Amar'e Stoudamire run a pick and roll reminded me of everything I needed to know about being a human being. Fact. Before that, it was on the basketball court that I became white when suddenly everyone I was playing against was black. That was a hell of a thing to find out with no warning. I watched TV and rooted for Larry Bird's every failure. It was a way to make amends, a concession. One night, walking down the street, age twelve, I bumped into this kid—the most hyped prospect to come from my city—he said, "c'mere" and started counting off a stack of twenties. I said, "Where'd you get all that?" He laughed and said, "You have to aks, you'll never know." Roughly speaking, that's how many things felt in that period. There are stories. I can't remember half of them, but there are stories. It's not my memory that's failing, though, it's my eyes. Maybe because I read too much, everything outside the text is blurry to me. I see friends and they're as unformed in my vision as strangers. Until they get close. Then everything changes. I want to keep them where I can see them. This is not figurative. This is literal. I bought a pair of glasses in Korea, where I had a job and stack of paper won. I wear the same glasses now, but they barely help, as every year some clarity is lost. This is a slow decline I'm riding, and though I'm resting my knee today it hurts anyway. When my wife and I were once lost in the Mt. Hood Wilderness Area and the sun had gone down, there was a part of me that hoped we'd have to spend the night sleeping under a tree by the river, just us and no one else to make it through. I used to say to girls, "I don't want to go down on you." God, the things I didn't understand. The things I don't. Things I won't. Not even *why*, I don't need a *why*, I'm happy with just because, but a *how* would be nice. I was a scientist once, after all. I lose sleep trying to reconcile form and emptiness. I remind myself they are two sides of the same coin, but this analogy's cash-value is debatable. I want to get off the coin altogether. I'm not there. The time between sleeping and waking is a total mind-fuck on those nights I'm able to track it. Trying to track who is tracking who is even worse. I want to tell you what I know, to contribute something worthy. Every eight weeks I give blood and when the needle pierces my vein I do not look away. I am fascinated. I watch as I am emptied. You are owed something by me. Take it. Please, take it. There are no rules. We will make some. You and I will figure out how to live. We will consult Aristotle and other sources, but we will not be beholden to them. The problem of authority is inescapable for me, a reluctant moralist. I wonder if I should be a moralist or not, but I've already said *should*. I am godless. I am not giving up. A religious man with no religion. God has been dead for some time now, but this news stays news. This generation outside of time, fighting to regress as far as progress will allow. Here I am, tired, confused, not as young as I once was, desperate. I want to raise a kid, but am fearful of what I'd teach her and the world that would happen to her. Here I am asserting my right to speak *while* struggling to listen. I want to make judgments. Good ones.

LISTS

books currently on upper right shelf of bookcase

1. *Changing My Mind*
2. *Everything Matters*
3. *I Am Not Sidney Poitier*
4. *Leaving the Atocha Station*
5. *Lit*
6. *n+1: Eleven*
7. *n+1: Twelve*
8. *Out of Sheer Rage*
9. *Where Men Win Glory*
10. *Whorled*

ways to drink coffee

1. with friends
2. alone
3. black
4. in a cafe
5. in Portland
6. cold, tired, dying (see *living*)
7. in the morning
8. reading Sartre
9. writing poetry
10. late at night

reasons to memoir

1. to tell truth
2. to discover more useful lies
3. to escape from under past
4. to connect with hypothetical other
5. narcissism (or: Facebook not cutting it)
6. to save lives (readers and/or own)

7. fear of insubstantiation
8. as practice of self-discovery
9. as practice of self-creation
10. to make real (concretize)

best Dylan albums (alphabetized)

1. *Another Side of Bob Dylan*
2. *Blonde on Blonde*
3. *Blood on the Tracks*
4. *Bringing It All Back Home*
5. *Highway 61 Revisited*
6. *Infidels*
7. *Modern Times*
8. *Planet Waves*
9. *The Times They Are A-Changin'*
10. *Time Out of Mind*

reasons to list

1. specificity/concision
2. accessibility
3. expedience
4. false impression of innocence
5. to make hard decisions (see *Oh Mercy, Desire, "Love and Theft,"* etc.)
6. to say what you want without having to name it
7. to reveal yet remain cryptic
8. laziness
9. pragmatism
10. to satisfy urge to categorize

some themes

1. reading/writing (art, generally)
2. selfhood (and other self- terms)
3. communication
4. death
5. creativity
6. perspective
7. memory/memoir
8. identity

9. Nietzsche
10. wonder

injuries

1. tendonitis (starting too soon)
2. Baker's cyst (current, ongoing)
3. bruised spine (cause: too embarrassing to name)
4. broken tibia (sister's)
5. hyper-extended knee (recovered)
6. concussions (2) (recovered?)
7. ITBS (not IBS, at least for now)
8. stitches on face (3 times, 12 total stitches)
9. stitches on left hand (3 times, 19 total stitches)
10. miscellaneous others (self-imposed one way or another)

varieties of blue

1. baby
2. black and
3. cheese
4. eyes
5. *Kind of*
6. Mountains
7. royal
8. s
9. self-portrait
10. sky

things in day bag (currently)

1. day planner
2. gum
3. highlighter
4. notebooks (2)
5. pencil
6. pens (3)
7. *The Chronology of Water*
8. *The Gay Science*
9. *What Narcissism Means to Me*
10. a million optimisms

REFLECTIONS

What we know about ourselves and remember is not so decisive for the happiness of our life as people suppose. One day that which others know about us (or think they know) assaults us—and we realize that this is more powerful. It is easier to cope with a bad conscience than to cope with a bad reputation.

—Nietzsche

Neighborhood Friend: I knew him since we were kids, mostly through sports. Even though we lived a block apart, we went to different schools. But we played soccer, baseball, and basketball together. This last, most importantly. My dad always told me to keep an eye on a guy with that much confidence. There was something about S. where if he decided to do something he just did it. He didn't ask permission, and he didn't talk about it too much either. And if he wanted you to join him, you would. He had that kind of charisma when he wanted to. But it was draining in a way. He was hard, is the only way I can think to say it, and he wanted you to be hard too. And if you weren't . . . sometimes you needed a break, but demanding as he was, you had to respect him.

Little League Baseball Coach: What a shame. No kid I ever coached played the game the way S. played. Plenty of kids were better, but no one else had that combination of ability, intelligence, creativity, and willingness to put forth effort. The old baseball cliché would be that he played the game the right way, but that's what he did. I don't remember a game ending when he wasn't bleeding or bruised and hadn't done at least one thing I wrote down to try to get across to the other players. It's strange how some things make an impact. And for him to just walk away like that. I'll never understand. I think there was always too much going on in his head. That was his problem.

Ex-girlfriend: I remember this time we went to the beach to stay with friends in a cabin. It was stormy out, and everyone was inside playing cards and drinking. At one point, all twelve or fifteen of us sat on the floor in a circle and began playing spoons—that's the game that's like musical chairs: there's one more player than spoon, and each round the person who doesn't get a spoon when someone makes a set of four is "out." Well, we were going along, and I got "out" about halfway through the game. Bad luck, I thought. But then I started watching S., and I started to notice something—maybe I'm reading too much into this because I know him and what some of his interests were in those days, but—he was playing very fast but without hurrying. Does that make sense? It was like he knew he was going to win before the game started, and he was just waiting for it to happen. There is skill to the game—you have to pay attention to everyone, so you can get a spoon quickly when the time comes, but in the end when there are two players and one spoon it's mostly a matter of hoping you're the first to draw four of a kind. So here's the punch line: S. won without a set of four; he was so focused that he read the other player's face and grabbed the spoon first when he (the other player) got a set. That's the only time I've seen that.

High School Basketball Coach: S.? I always thought he was overrated. I had these two assistants who kept telling me to give him a chance, that he was the point guard I was looking for. C'mon. He had some skills, sure, but my niece has skills too. You have to think about who he was going up against. Put him on the court against some of those black kids and they would have run circles around him. He was too slow and his shot was too inconsistent. I'll put it real simple: there's a thing called *it* and he just didn't have it. You think somebody who has *it* joins the chess club?

High School Chess Coach: S. was my best student. He came to the game late and that limited what he was able to do, but for those few years he made drastic improvements and played some beautiful games. Plus just having him involved gave the chess team a little status we didn't have before. Is that enough?

School Friend: Me and S. go way back. School and sports back to elementary days. Baseball, hoops, soccer, street hockey, tennis, everything really. We were both smart, both popular, both good athletes. We were friends sometimes, best friends sometimes, rivals sometimes, kind of moved around in a normal way. There was always this side, though, where he'd go off in his head somewhere and it was like, I don't know, he became kind of inaccessible. I think it causes him suffering—but I don't know if he'd ever give it up either. What are you gonna do?

Artist Friend: I was kind of awkward in middle school, and S. was the first cool person I was friends with. That's a funny thing to say now, because he's pretty far removed from the things that made him cool in high school, but that's the thing, he's always been out ahead a little bit from where everyone else is at—or if not actually ahead, kind of on his own somewhere. So at the end of sophomore year he was the person who first got me drunk and high and took me to parties and introduced me to girls and all that. Nowadays, he likes to live a pretty quiet life with the Mrs., but something at the core is still the same, and I'm damn thankful for that thing.

Wife: Something that made S. different from other guys was his intensity and his confidence. He made his intentions clear and didn't apologize for them. His directness was uncommon for our age at the time, and I didn't know how to react at first, but I think we both knew that our being together was inevitable. There was this palpable feeling that when he approached me that first night our futures were already sealed.

Friend (?): To this day I don't know what to make of S. We were friends. In a way we still are friends, but, God, I don't know where to start. Maybe someone else should do this?

Former Friend: Well, he stole my girlfriend. Did he tell you that? Came over to my place, drank my beer, watched my TV, took my girl. He had it all, too, but it wasn't enough, he had to take the only thing I had. Jesus, that was a low point. Ah, well, it was a long time ago now and my life is good, not that I'll forget though. Be careful with him, he'll probably try to spin this like it wasn't his fault: love can't be denied, learning experience, something.

High School Cross Country Coach: Anyone who knows me knows I always see the best in my kids, but I'll do my best to keep to the facts here. I got great kids every year. That's why I loved my job. Just getting out there and working hard and having fun. S. was one of the good ones. He was above average and a hard worker. A good kid. Nothing special, talent-wise. He was the best runner in his year, but his year was one of the weakest, especially compared to all the talent ahead and behind him. Still, I liked S., and he was good to have around. He had more talent and less work ethic in class probably than he did in sports, but he never caused much trouble except maybe paying a little too much attention to the girls. Can't blame him for that, though.

Dad: I can't talk about my son without talking about my father.

Mom: S.'s dad was in a car accident when S. was about a year and a half old. He was hit by a drunk driver. The car seat was in the car and was ejected through a window. The witnesses were sure the baby was dead, but when they ran to the seat they saw it was empty, there was no one there. I've told S. he was lucky his dad didn't die in that accident because I never could have raised him on my own. He was an explosive child. He was stronger than me mentally and when he unleashed his rage, nearly as strong physically. I don't know where that rage came from. It had to be from his dad, though, because only he could get S. under control—and it took quite a toll on him to do it. It scares me, actually, to think what would have become of him. His sister I could have raised okay alone. But, S., there's just no way.

Mentor: One thing to keep in mind about S. is his inclination to self-mythologize. It's a very American aspect to him, this particular kind of exceptionalism. It's like everyone else is merely playing a role in the story of Great S.! He's too intelligent to finally believe that sort of thing, but he's intrigued by how he is—and how people in general are—drawn to feel that way. It's one of the things that works in his memoir, where he's constantly negotiating the back and forth between self-mythologizing, which is of course a kind of self-deception and real self-understanding.

Religious Friend: I think [Mentor] is right that S. wouldn't finally believe in any kind of exceptionalism, except isn't there a performative contradiction occurring here. I mean, here he is literally writing the words we're saying about him, literally making us characters in his story. What could be more controlling, more solipsistic?

Brother-in-law: Someone probably needs to come in here and say that without even getting into questions about the purpose of drawing attention to the solipsism of this project (or any project oriented around the nature of selfhood), and whether that's a comment on the nature and (un)reality and (im)possibility, which is to say contradiction(s), of subjectivity, on a simpler level this conversation is just a convenient—and when you think about it, pretty direct way—of communicating what it's like to be his I, right? What's more fundamental to S.'s own personal I than how he thinks others see him?

Linguist Friend: And while there is an enormous kind of meta-confirmation bias at work here, who gets to speak (and who doesn't) is telling in its own right.

Pretty Much Everyone: Frankly, I've never thought much about him. He always struck me as being kind of boring. He doesn't talk much, just gives off the impression that he's tolerating you and would rather be off by himself somewhere. I don't know if he's Romantic or Great or whatever. It's possible. It's also possible he's just a loner. And in either case, misunderstood artists, depression, who cares? I'm so over that.

Music Friend: We used to go to Elliott Smith concerts together—

Lots of People, in unison: Figures.

Music Friend: Anyway . . . you think it's obvious now, but at the time it meant something for him to go to those shows and participate in that scene. He didn't have to. In fact, no one expected him to. But he saw that there was something there and that it was worth something. I think he was reaching, even if he didn't know what for.

College Professor: I once told S. he was the smartest student I'd ever had, but man he was he resistant to learning. He went about things his own way, and if that way was going to dead end, he wouldn't turn around till he hit that wall himself. It's not the most efficient way to learn, but it's very sincere. And when I reflect now with a little distance it seems obvious that he was far from the smartest student, but he took things very seriously, and there's something impressive about his resolution and the depth of his feeling—in fact, I'd call that an accomplishment, an intelligence, in its own right.

College Friend: We were both into Buddhism in those days. We meditated, read sutras, and took classes. I don't know what self S. was trying to get out from under. He either didn't really have one or he kept it pretty well tucked away. Or maybe that malleability, that manipulative tendency even, was the essential part. I'm not the one to say. For all the time we spent together, all the interest we shared, I never knew him, not really. I hope he's well.

Wife's Friend: I thought he was sketchy for a long time, but what I've come to see is that he's playing a different game than most of us. He can be intimidating, but he doesn't mean anything by it. It's the price he pays for what he's trying to be. He's trying very hard, I think, to do good.

Grad School Friend: I was S.'s best friend in the program. From pretty much the time we met it felt like we'd always known each other. I don't know too much about his past because we always had so much present between us. I've learned this, though: if you ask S. a question he'll answer it, and if you want to know what he has to say you better listen because he doesn't like to repeat himself. And if you don't ask him he probably won't tell you. He's sort of strangely content that way to just be. It's funny he's a memoirist, when you think about it. Always confessing but never revealing. He's quite diligent as well, though I never can tell if that feels like pressure to him. I've always known him, but I still don't know him, if that makes any sense.

Cousin: Yeah, that's how it is for me too. I just can't figure out how to get at his essence. Sometimes when I read something he's written, I feel closer to him, but then I put the book down and it slips away again. Even when we're together, I feel like there's a basic absence in him, some kind of abyss I've never been able to penetrate. I'd like to know what's in there.

Sister: I probably know what it's like for S. to be S. better than anyone, and I admire what he's trying to do.

ALL CRITICISM IS AUTOBIOGRAPHICAL

A: Did I plagiarize you? Meaning borrowed meaning stole meaning knew a good thing when I saw it?

B: Can two people plagiarize each other at the same time? Meaning a copy circle meaning a figure eight meaning a jinx?

A: Telepathy and inspiration work in nurtureable ways.

B: This is not about how to translate but rather what translation does, and conversely, what it does not do.

A: All criticism is autobiography. Dig yourself. Stokely Carmichael.

B: Translation does, in a literal sense, substitute the original source, but it doesn't supplant it.

A: An artist chooses his subjects; that is his way of praising. Nietzsche.

B: You should write a memoir that quotes your reviews—and maybe other sources too.

The journey's purpose is to correct the trajectory of life and lead to a better version of self. . . . It's with a writer's impulse toward narrative that the hike is given such significance before its inception. The road is less about adventure than an opportunity for observation and reflection. What does it mean to be a man now, here—in America? He is on a search for success, authenticity, self-approval, and happiness. . . . He sometimes sounds like he's so comfortable with searching that if he ever found success or happiness it would be a letdown. When he gets there, he finds what he always finds: margins to live in, self-improvements to forgo, and mistakes to make. "No man's land" describes . . . places where people are cut off from themselves. She's as devastatingly honest with herself as she is with the rest of us, and she resists the easy finger-pointing solutions and identifies her own self-misunderstanding.

It would be disingenuous of him to pretend for very long his mind isn't made up, for when the data and observations start coming in, it's pretty obvious where he's heading. What he does instead is to report on his own feelings in the same disinterested tone he uses to report on, say, feces in our meat being called a "cosmetic blemish." Unfortunately, the honest, reflective voice that makes her such a capable memoirist occasionally lets her down as a theologian. The epistemology of the religious is that a criticism . . . is wrong not because it is logically flawed, but because it is a criticism. The conversation appears to be over before it's begun. He is honest and fair and empathetic. He gives voice to all the people he writes about, so each position receives its strongest articulation. When he points out weaknesses in the arguments, he does so with respect. The problem is not the experience. The problem is that, because we lack alternatives, these experiences are held up to support religious worldviews. As a general rule, people who have made intentional decisions are more articulate about their conclusions than those who come across their positions accidentally. Developing or locating a workable worldview for oneself is a fundamental human responsibility, and one that is perhaps felt most acutely by apostates. Having sacrificed religious certainty, he embraces his limited understanding. But such acceptance doesn't come easily. Buddhism stripped of all supernatural elements is among the best approaches our species has yet developed in response to the problem of finding meaning and flourishing in this world.

Not one, normally, to over-editorialize his observations, he allows his recurring pessimism onto the page. In a line of thinking he borrows from Marx, he shows how the division of labor that makes our efficiency and wealth possible is also responsible for the alienation of the modern worker. The real fun of this book, as is the fun of all Dylan books, is that its stories lead back to the music—the wonderful, perplexing music, the relentlessly contemporary music, the heart-crumpling and spirit-invigorating music, the incomprehensibly vast music. Vague as Dylan has often been about his life, and synthetic as his body of work is (of voices, of times, of traditions, of musical styles), we have to strain to imagine a post-Civil War America without him, even though we know there was one and will be another. Popular music follows from these conditions—we see artists like Dylan and Eminem reach levels of success far beyond those of the black artists their works are modeled on. Hip hop has become the soundtrack of our car commercials; the letdown of its cultural ubiquity is that its rebelliousness and criticisms have been widely absorbed by the mainstream. Money never sleeps, but morality might sneak an occasional nap. . . . That co-option is even possible on such a scale evinces the very subversion of idealism to market realism that is at stake. The seduction of rebelling against the strictures of society by *self-indulgence* eventually came to dominate the intention of rebelling against the strictures of society by *practicing an intentionally idealistic lifestyle*. While so many people really don't know how to live, their particular brand of not knowing is unique and compelling.

Invariably, these approaches say more about their authors than about the topic at hand, and Dylan becomes a mere springboard for the author to demonstrate the applicability of his or her perspective. For readers who are willing to put forth the effort to follow the philosophy, it is fairly accessible, as are most of the essays that precede it in the book. . . . And when the logic gets technical, the intelligibility of the examples makes it possible to track the argument. (This is a memoir with an argument.) But proof is always secondary to experience, and abstraction must be earned; once earned, it might grant one the privilege to view history from a remove. This method of dismantling cold intellectualism through a combination of better intellection and complete sincerity—which follows directly from his uniquely generous and hostile refutation of Taylor's "Fatalism" (I'll grant all your premises and then I'll just flat-out out argue you)—will be one of Wallace's lasting contributions to American letters.

In short: he is without the benchmarks of traditional rights of passage into adult masculinity. His identity is an amorphous, insubstantial thing. And while being freed from the societal roles men have faced is wildly liberating, it can be equally paralyzing. One of the preoccupations of a memoir—and one of the form's strengths—is its attempt to account for the narrative self: whence the "I" on this page? The question is interrogated across the full span of life . . . as the author eventually embraces who she is—and what she can and can't do. Of course, the mind's impulse to create stories and to compress information for meaning means details are squeezed from memory. Little in this world is real, and what is might be made unreal at any moment. Many of the recurring images here focus on what's not present. The lyrical flourishes occasionally overreach, but when they hit their mark they hit it true. The emergence of the subject's self (shaped as it still is by childhood circumstances) plays out in the book's narration as well.

It's a committed attempt at self-destruction, and one of the author's triumphs is to cop to the intentionality of this obliterating urge rather than present his addiction as simply a case of pursuing pleasure too far. It's only in Endings, as an adult, his parents dead or dying, that he seems freed from the guilt of imperfection. But this is also when, thanks to his writing, he's become the kind of hard worker his parents or God might respect. One of the novel's major themes is living with the consequences of one's choices. . . . But individual agency is largely subsumed by wider forces. History is fate and he is adept at pointing out the ironies fate produces. Where there is freedom to pursue happiness, there is "lifelessness and defeatism. Indiscriminate weariness [is] prevalent."

Anyone looking for a straight recovery memoir will be disappointed. First-person narration is given secondary weight to a third-person exposition of philosophy, psychology, and neurology. But even the third-person account is less focused on . . . shaking in particular than on the history of the mind/body dualism in general. The author circles her subject, getting at it from different angles, struggling to find an elusive *cause*. But the story of causation constantly demands retelling; there's always more to be said, a factor that's been ignored. The book is ultimately searching for a cohesive narrative of her *self*. She circles and circles because there's no way to go right at this issue. The mind-body relationship is the black hole at the center of consciousness and it lurks behind all stories—the stories we read and the stories we all call "I."

The formula he has created is to select a subject and then show (more than argue) how it's relevant to our lives and deserving of our thoughtful attention. The meta-lite style in which she presents herself is indicative of two of her primary concerns: the *I* on the page, which "is only a convenient term for somebody who has no real being"; and the very real (heaps and heaps of being) author who scripts *I*. The narrative of the writing of the narrative is necessary for her to profess the distinction between the author, on the one hand, and the voice on the page, on the other. Unlike many philosophers—and one of the main reasons he is often considered not a "real" one—he takes the risk of making himself understood. But his project is more essayistic than anything else. For a writer who communicates his meanings so cleanly, it is striking that the biggest fault in his latest book lies not in something he said but in something he didn't.

The interest both of these share in freeing the human subject from the strictures of language mirrors the personal shift from academic philosophy that challenges the minds of very few readers to the literature with which he provokes the hearts and minds of a great many readers—readers who, thanks to him, might just learn how to better shape their own futures. On a meta-level, what it does is much more important. It reveals not the correct or final interpretation but the value of interpretation itself. The book's bold aspiration is to be that rare hybrid, the academic work urgent enough to change the reader's life. The primary character . . . sometimes feels like she's being externally manipulated, and even fears she's a character in a book. The authors repeatedly pierce the book's seal to open it up from itself. Like friends, books are always in service of self-cultivation, always leading us on to our future selves, always reminding us to put them down.

First of all, he makes the joy of running palpable. The argument for running closer to our natural state is finding traction among runners. It's an argument that will find sympathetic ears in Michael Pollan's readership and other groups who see that who we've been has relevance for who we are, and the longer we've lived a certain way the wiser we would be to trust there's a reason for it. Far back in our evolutionary past, one of the key attributes that allowed our species to excel was our ability to run; we evolved because we could run, and therefore we evolved *to run*. His accidental encounter led the author to wonder why "they all seem so damn happy." But perhaps more striking is the amount and kind of meaning these athletes draw from their sport.

Again and again, the things these runners say about running center around friendship, learning, self-acceptance, and happiness. Health for them is as much mental, spiritual, and emotional as it is physical. These runners all participate in *the joy of running qua running*, a jovial state of running wherein the experience of running becomes its sole purpose. It's such an admirable goal—imploring us to reengage with our bodies for the sake of our lives—that the reader roots for the conclusions, and is inspired to follow her recommendations for individuals, gentle and achievable as they are. Hiking the Oregon section of the trail is appropriate, as Portland is where she plans to live once she's off the trail. Though her plan for self-recreation is highly determined, the execution is so haphazard and improvisational that she is led to some truly unexpected moments that are worthy of the psychological burden she's put on them. It's a fearless story, told in honest prose that is wildly lyrical as often as it is dirtily physical.

What do we value more, our morals or our pleasure and convenience? . . . How much do we care about what we care about? Enough to change? Readers will recognize their own dependencies on consumer culture and infer the full range of its perversions. The despair for the legacy we're leaving our future generations might make for a dispiriting read. The issue at stake is the interaction between humans and the other 3–30 million (and crashing) animals that share this planet. . . . attempts to make us care about animals by breaking down the dichotomies we rely on to hold up the distinction between human and non-, dichotomies like which animals are capable of play, gustatory pleasure, companionship, and love. Whatever the causes of an animal's behavior, there is still the question of the animal's subjective experience. Whether it's sea otters linking paws or a marmot sniffing flowers, one must be quite disciplined to have a first response of "that looks like a survival strategy" rather than "they look happy." One of the real knock-down arguments for animals enjoying pleasure for pleasure's sake comes from the wild ubiquity of homosexual and autoerotic sex, most famously in female bonobos, who "engage in a bout of GG rubbing [clitoris on clitoris] about once every two hours." There are worse readings of our species's history than to say those with power have tended to exercise it against those without. Empathy is prerequisite to morality, so just look at those seals in love. Just look. The author reads the mangrove fiasco in economic terms, too, identifying the market's failure to account for its environmental destruction that it writes off as an externality. Of course, while destroying an ecosystem may be external to any given balance sheet, it's not external the life of a single person on this planet. What if saving, say, tigers is a net cost rather than a net gain—should we let them die? Is that the kind of world we want to live in?

Rhetorically, an inspirational sendoff is expected here. But we already know in essence, what they ask: sacrifice in some form, and compassion. It will be hard and it might not succeed. Of course, this declaration is both true and not true. We need those bees—desperately—but in a world where good intentions can feel insignificant, poetry might be one of the things that can sustain us and make the world worth its inheritors. Nature . . . is the refuge of last resort in times of grief as well as in times of meaninglessness. As an experienced nature-goer, she knows to slow down amidst her explorations enough that she really notices and engages her surroundings, which allows her to reflect abstractly and insightfully on what she sees. ("Rain that fell like dead weight all winter long defies gravity in the spring." Do people not from Oregon know how accurate this is?) What she is offering here is a vision of what she calls the "secular sacred". . . . when we take the time to notice, there's so much to be thankful for.

He is feeling the all-too-human longing that fatalism might sometimes be as un-true with respect to the past as we assume it is with respect to the future. There are no answers out there, he intuits; the ocean, the open road ahead, your father, your country—nothing can relieve the burden of having to form one's own identity. The project of becoming a man is never complete, and so the chronicle of that journey can never finally be written. The incomplete story the book tells, then, is the story of its own creation: the story of the narrator coming into being as a man, as a man embracing the project of his own self-becoming. In our post-Nietzschean world, human life comes burdened with the need to account for itself—a neces-sity made urgent by the looming and "inevitable" promise of death. So the solace comes not from escaping the specter of death for the length of an entertaining book, or from reading self-assuring promises that no writer is in any position to make, but from the satisfaction that comes from seeking truth. One writer's deliberation over whether to be tested for the lethal Huntington's disease (a rare hereditary condition he had 50/50 odds on), demands us to imagine what we'd do if our chances of survival were 50/50—and to think about what we will do since our chances *are* zero. It's an informative read, simultaneously inspiring and real-istic—and one any young idealist should be sure to note.

UNANSWERED QUESTIONS?

How is this possible? How is anything
possible? For example, how is it that I'm
here at all? How is it possible that I'm out
of beer already? How am I my father's son?
How is he his? Or: How am I my author's
creation? How am I my creation's author?
How are these hands the hands I was
born with? Can they touch the past? Why
so much introspection? What good is it doing
me? Where do you go when you sleep? Where
were you before you were born? Where will you go
when you die? How can we let death not
force upon us life? How can it not absolve fear?
What are we holding on to? What would happen if we
let go? What are we so scared of?
How is it possible that form and emptiness
are two sides of the same coin? To return
to basics: why is there something rather than
nothing? Over all these eons, what have we gained?
Do you like silence as much as I like silence?
How do some people sleep at night? How
do they get through the day? What little stories,
what lies, do they comfort themselves with?
Are their lies like my lies? Am I a destiny?
Are you? Was Nietzsche, really? Does it matter?
To whom? What's the difference between morality
and moralism? Why can't I let sleeping dogs
lie? If you wake the dogs then will you let them lie?
Why is truth so painful? Is there truth
or just stories? Why does asking questions
so often lead to unhappiness? What good advice
do you regularly ignore? What price do you pay
for the advice you do follow? Is it worth it? Why
is happiness so bound up with thoughtlessness? Why
is thoughtlessness both admirable and detestable? Why
is the grass always greener? Is the grass always greener?

Here is grass between my fingers—do you want this grass?
Why does prayer work for atheists? Is there worse news
for an atheist than that prayer works, works meaning helps,
helps meaning relieves, relieves meaning opens, opens
meaning love, love meaning love meaning meaning—
anything worse? Is that a serious question?
Do you know that Elliott Smith lyric "I'm never
gonna know you now / but I'm gonna love
you anyhow"? By what world-historical forces
do you know or not know, feel or not feel, that lyric?
Why is the connection between Elliott Smith and
David Foster Wallace so rarely remarked upon? Shall
we draw the comparisons? Would you sacrifice
truth for happiness, happiness for truth? Do you know
yet that you will be asked to sacrifice? Do you know
that this is one of those instances where not answering
is itself an answer? What will you choose? Are you
as paralyzed by the various flavors of ice cream as I am?
With every flavor available to us, how do we choose
what to order, let alone how to love? Why does acting
unselfishly for selfish reasons still make you less selfish?
If thinking changes action and action changes thinking,
why don't we consolidate and just say *living*? Why worry
so much? Are you, in fact, a worrier? Can you help it?
Are you not who you are? Is that the meaning of *are*?
How does it feel? No really, how does it feel?
Would you rather I asked you something else? What
question could I ask that would make you happy? Is
happiness what is needed right now? Which happiness
is your happiness? How do you choose? How do you choose
what to choose by? How do you choose what to choose
what to choose by? How did anyone ever get off
the ground? Is this what they mean by *logical*? Which
of these questions have answers? And which
of these questions have questions? What happens
to you when you focus really hard on infinity? If
I asked you to be quiet, could you be quiet? If I asked you
to walk, would you be able to move your feet? If I asked you
a question, would you answer it? If I needed your help,
would you help me? If I offered you my help, would you
accept it? Would you trust me? Do you trust
the intentions of your makers of things? Have we really
come so far? Should we even ask if we should be thinking

about going back? Is it too late for that question? Too soon?
Have you been to Disney Land? Have you read Baudrillard?
Are you able to function despite it all? How is your nostalgia
reconciled? Or is it? Do you believe in narrative? Do your narratives
care about your beliefs? What do you have that won't leave
you, or when do you feel like you're not left with nothing?
What is the nothing of nothing? Do you wonder what
your own words mean? When you read a phrase
like "the nothing of nothing," which variety of nothing
comes to mind and how generous do you want to be
in this moment? Should it be left alone? Is that your considered opinion?
Is nihilism as unlikely as everything else? Can you elaborate
on the difference between something and nothing? Why
would I ask that? What is it I want from you? Do you
require your own answers? Who do you give your answers
to? In the face of certain annihilation, what are your priorities?
Do you feel sometimes already annihilated? How often
do you think about annihilation? Is it wonderful?
Is there anything greater? Can you imagine living
without it? The horror of that? Certain annihilation
in the dead center of your mind, what were those priorities?
Can I see it on your face? Does it trouble you? Are you
troubled? Which responsibilities do you take, and which ones
do you leave behind? Do you ever curse Nietzsche late at night?
How strong are you? What is the greatest test you've ever
passed? Failed? How would you respond if I asked you
what you are capable of? Do you know, or would you
need some time? Do you believe that you learn about
someone by finding out what they deny themselves?
Or should I ask what thoughts you deny yourself?
Can you make do with less? Can you withstand
more? What is your vision? Who and what
will you not let stand in your way? Do you still think
some stories are not stories at all? If I said I wanted
to get past stories, to get to what's beneath them,
how would you respond? That you don't know
what I mean? That you and I have nothing in common?
That I'm wasting my time? That didn't my grandma tell me
not to think so much? That those questions don't lead
anywhere? That humans are humans? That inadequacy
is its own (and the only real) inadequacy? That this is war?
That somewhere birds are flying? That this is for the birds
that are somewhere flying? That tragedy is a matter of

perspective? That nothing matters but everything? That
everything is everything? That that includes stories and survival?
That questions don't have to have answers, can be their own
answers? If I said I'm just curious, would you believe me?
How do you respond? Will you, in the end, actually
respond? Please? What if adult sanity means giving
and getting responses? What if it means knowing
when enough is enough? Have you ever met one,
do they exist, these sane adults? If you meet one,
what will you ask?

WILL TO AGENCY

My waking life begins on a Tuesday when a stranger asks what's the story?
and I say there's no story. It's just . . . moments, an accretion of moments

Stranger: I'm familiar with this story.

S.:   Fleeting emotions, passing thoughts, desires, instincts, et cetera.
         Don't forget the et cetera.

Stranger: So you're in it.

S.:   Sure, so are you. I'm kind of reading it as I write. It's like I'm all
         the time sort of inside it.

         I know what you mean.

The day I found out that my cousin killed himself looks like this: S. spends afternoon out in nature doing nature things with woman. Woman drops S. off at sister's house. S. says to sister hi. Sister knows something S. doesn't know and can't face him. S. thinks he has interrupted a fight and turns to sister's boyfriend and says what's up? Sister's boyfriend mumbles mumbles and leaves. S. has been in nature with woman and is happily oblivious. He sees his phone and that Dad has called. There is no precedent for this. S. sees that Dad has in fact called twice. S. calls Dad. Dad says have you heard? S. says heard what? Dad says Jason is dead. S. says what do you mean? Dad repeats. S. repeats. Dad says suicide. S. says what do you mean? S. says I'll call you back. S. stands, looks around, doesn't know where to go, where the fuck to go. He must go. He goes out where there is wet Oregon grass and spring light and he must feel it and his legs are weak and he goes down in it and he weeps and he rolls his face in the grass and weeps and cries out and weeps.

[lapse of indeterminate length of time]

This going is not enough go.

S. goes to sister. Brother and sister hug and cry and do not speak.

S. calls woman from nature.

It is night now.

They go to S.'s bed and S. cries and they make love under a blanket of darkness.

It is slow and it is gentle.

It is love and it is necessary.

* * *

The thought currently passing again through the currents of my past is the distorted repetition that is the inception of originality: a mutated copy of a copied mutation. That cloud enmeshed in the fog of my inner milieu is the pesky memetic reminder that I'm not so much living a life as writing a history so I'll have something to read when I go around looking for things like causes. Causes, urges for:

I wrote all of this and I wrote none of this.

It's life and death,

and the space between

is genitals

rubbing

on genitals

to make more life and death

to be filled

with more rubbing genitals

to make

to one day make

to one day maybe make—

* * *

When infinite possibility is collapsed, it is collapsed to:

History, stones and bones, truths as unalterable as they are unknowable, regrets deserved and un-, opportunities realized and forgone—the inexorable facts of having been here fighting a losing battle. Contingency, of course, unconquerable.

And yet:

More fresh starts, more attempts to get going, more desperate pleas for momentum, more grasping, more anguish, more disappointment, more ego, more death, more will to agency, more more more—the irrepressible urge to narrate.

Fig. 2. Graphic representation of memoirist (with notes):

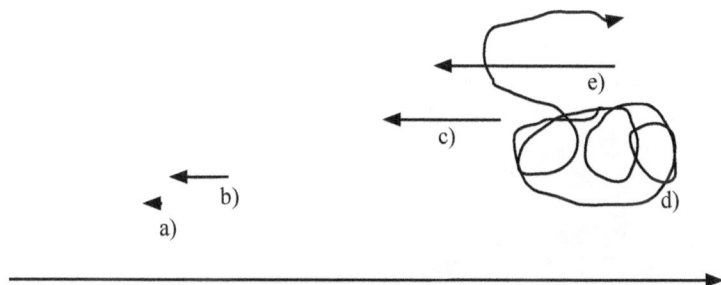

a) *The eighth day of the eighth month of the eighty-eighth year (20th-century C.E.) was a normal day, but that's when the damage was done.*

b) *This is the autobiography of the first eleven years of my life and some of the important people in them. The first person I want to talk about . . .*

c) *The events contained in this do not stand alone. They stand together only because I have put them into these words you're reading. But that is not the only story. Before that they were arranged differently, and alternatively, in various orders, emphasizing assorted other themes, for there were many revisions and many more edits. Prior to that, these events have been manipulated, organized, categorized, altered, doctored, touched up, remembered, forgotten, re-remembered, and indulged, in my mind. Prior still, these things all happened in the world of physical bodies and passing time. The here stated significance may have been co-present with the occurrences, but for the most part has been assigned in retrospect.*

d) *I'm always in the middle of it, always kind of circling it, grasping at it, never feeling like I'm quite getting at it. It, it, it, it's right in front of me. I can almost make it out. I can put my hands around it, squeeze it, use it—it has a use: it puts together, assembles, combines, unifies the apart, the unassembleable, the components, the individuals—makes them one, a thing, an artifact with an identity, a genealogy, even an essence.*

e) *I come out to Minnesota hot on Bob Dylan's trail.*

* * *

Which parts add up to a convincing whole? Who is being convinced?

I want to read a book that has it all. Everything. What would that look like? I want to at least start the first sentence. What is the first sentence? Who would write that sentence? How do you conceive of God when every god you can conceive of answers nothing? Why does solving problems feel like an effective use of time? Why not make problems and accept that it's time that uses me?

Thrown from the ether, submerged, I'm trying to teach myself how to swim from the inside, swim so well I become the water and breathe the water.

POLYVOCAL MONOLOGUE OF A VEXED SELF

Henry James: Autobiography may be the preeminent kind of American expression.

Author: Our preoccupations with self-reliance and self-creation.

Montaigne: It is not my deeds that I write down, it is myself, my essence.

Author: Our preoccupation with self.

Clive James: Sick of being a prisoner of my childhood, I want to put it behind me.

Author: Sick of being myself, I want to write a better one.

Karen Armstrong: We should probably all pause to confront our past from time to time, because it changes its meaning as our circumstances alter.

Author: I trust no man who does not walk alone in the woods from time to time.

David Ben-Gurion: Anyone who believes you can't change history has never tried to write his memoirs.

Author: Or put himself to sleep at night.

Aristotle: Happiness is the meaning and the purpose of life, the whole aim and end of human existence.

Author: Happiness is a one-word tautology. Life's only purpose is death. Meanwhile we write past and future with imagination.

Solon: Let no man be called happy before his death.

Author: Let no man be called man before his book is written; but let no man write no book.

Barthes: The text is a tissue of quotations drawn from the innumerable centres of culture.

Author: Let man kill himself a thousand times and never die.

Barthes: To give a text an Author is to impose a limit on that text, to furnish it with a final signified, to close the writing.

Author: And let the books write themselves.

SOLIPSISMCIZED

Notes for writing this chapter:

- pick up on theme that self can never be completely represented, is never itself complete

- it's kind of the central thesis for the collection: the problems of self-identity, self-representation, self-understanding, really any hyphenated noun that's first term is "self-," ends in contradiction (ricocheting back and forth between absolute nothingness and infinite regress) because it begins in contradiction and cannot escape it, given that the escape would have to be contra-contradiction, which at best would leave diction, which exists only against non-diction—and so we're still trapped: circle is expanded slightly but we're still trapped: the discord appears as soon as we open our mouths

- there's no outside from which to look back or look in, by definition

- therefore there's no real objectifying possibility, therefore the tyranny of the subjective, therefore trapped (Try to avoid this conclusion, though.)

- Perfection Kills.

- Don't open your mouth. And don't not open your mouth. Jump!

- given that these problems are unsolvable, if they are unsolvable, there is still the question of what to do, right? even if we can't think our way out of our condition, we still live in the condition, right? so, where do we go from here? do we have to go somewhere?

- related, this is the one where I think about how writing about the self necessarily makes one (me) (more) self-involved, despite the fact that I think the point of art is to lead beyond the self

- explain how art does this (*how does art do this?*)

- there's a reader *and* a writer (remember this distinction (!) it seems important and may crop up again later)

- something to ask: does writing about oneself further isolate the self by sort of reinforcing it and drawing its perimeter? what happens if you cut at that perimeter? where are my scissors?

- is feeling despicable a byproduct of thinking about myself, and the kind of narcissism it requires corrosive to the soul? side effect to a kind of writing that might do good in other ways?

- i'm not as self-involved as this writing makes me feel—but i could write something else . . . maybe this writing is revealing something fundamental . . . maybe i'd suffer less if i . . . maybe the writing itself is the problem . . . maybe i need to keep going and find out what's on the other side . . . maybe i'll get there and maybe i won't . . . maybe if I were wise . . .

- there needs to be a reminder (in this section or another?) that there are parts of me that are better/healthier. i need to show for my sake and the writing's that i am peaceful, caring, calm, giving, generous, loving, whatever else, forgiving (need to make those things true)

- try to figure out if this is memoir—it's not supposed to be, but face the fact and the implications that maybe it is

- make clear the distinction that these are intellectual more than personal/emotional problems: they go away when i let them—most of the time

- when I ask "who am I?" it's not from a place of crisis, it's from a place of curiosity. what a bizarre (what a wildly fucking bizarre) situation to be aware of (incomprehensible!) and so in the end this ends in just saying "screw it, i can't figure this out," which is the real figuring it out—it's crazy stuff to think about, lots of kicks here, but at the end of the day: chop wood, carry water, etc.

- quote Issa? "What a strange thing! / to be alive / beneath cherry blossoms."

- the trick is going to be figuring out a way to kind of hint at or say all of this despite the obstacles of 1) not knowing if it's true; 2) not knowing if language is up to the task, or if i am—should i go right at, or is there a better angle of approach?

- these are old, old problems—Universal—but they're not boring because everyone faces them alone and anew—that's what Universal means

- try to get reader to see that there's a way out of this trap. is there a way out? try to get yourself to see that. whether the epistemology checks out or not, it's going to be productive (consider looking into pragmatism)

- it's becoming increasingly clear at this point that one of the fundamental questions is turning out to be where to come down on truth vs. happiness— for anyone who asks this question, instinct has got to be with the former. and damn if jealousy isn't riding shotgun.

- to not be debilitated by thought, to whatever else retain the ability to function, to survive—better, *to thrive*—to put the book down and live

- the same questions keep recurring in different forms, almost as if the conversation perpetuates itself. No more words. [move this chapter to end of collection??]

NARRATIVE THERAPY

Writing the first-person singular pronoun is associated with increased depression and self-destructive behavior. The only professional group with a higher rate of suicide than writers is dentists. Philosophers also commit suicide at a high rate. Among writers, poets are at greatest risk of suicide.

Three friends read this manuscript. One called it philosophy. One called it poetry. One called it fiction. I'm calling it nonfiction because I want to save people. Because the only reason I read and the only thing I read for is to be saved.
I don't read books to understand them; I read them to cannibalize them—I take only what I need and leave the rest to rot.

There is no not-improvising, no self not always emanating from self. I journaled off and on as a kid. In college I journaled for survival. After college, I started *writing* and have not journaled consistently since.

I have lost the ability to distinguish between my art and my life.

ME TOO

I

"Hello. Is there anyone out there?" I misremembered a song lyric, I can imagine myself saying from time to time, I think I do say, I think may be the only thing I ever say(s).

I, the only lonely pronoun.

I, homonym for the organ that lets the world in but can't shake the feeling that it's projecting out.

The missing   , an absence that informs—that's as close as I can get to rendering the strangeness of being in a body, oneself, in the world: always facing out.

David Foster Wallace said, "One of the things that makes Wittgenstein a real artist to me is that he realized that no conclusion could be more horrible than solipsism."

If you're reading this, you're out there. And I'm in here. Check the byline. S. it says. But I don't know if you're out there or not. And I'm not sure I'm really in here. S.? A stranger. *Je est un autre*. This whole thing? A farce.

I is. What else is there to say? I'm trying but I don't know where to go from here. No matter how many fragments of solitude I find, remember, imagine, invent, or steal, no matter how many ways I try to isolate the I, hovering all around the conceived, written, revised, read, is a lie with an *I* right in the middle of it.

My I is fragmented. How can I put it back together when I don't even recognize the pieces, when I'm not sure if they're from one set or a multitude, when I can't figure out if there's a final picture or just angles, perspectives.

I'm suddenly flashing back to a confused night when I tapped on a window for twenty minutes trying to get your attention before I realized I was standing in front of a mirror.

Oh my god. "What is art? Who am I?" Dar Williams once joked. Later, she covered a Pink Floyd song.

If there was no Other, I'd be forced to invent you.

I sometimes seems like one of those problems that I create for myself just by thinking about it. When I'm not thinking about, what's the problem? On the other hand, when I dig in and try to solve the problem once and for all, it sort of dissolves. Looking for I all I find is

I is a story I tell myself. A story tell myself. Tell myself a story.

I teased my wife one morning: "You don't know anything about me."
   She said, "I know your behavior."
   For a moment I felt totally exposed, for a moment I didn't exist.
   And then I came fully into melancholic existence, wishing her to be not only right but also exhaustive.
   So I wouldn't feel compelled to write words like these.
   So even if I wrote these same words, it would be just a peculiar behavior of mine.
   And I wouldn't feel like there was an essence I wasn't getting at, an isness of is I wasn't quite articulating.

II

I don't know what it's like inside you and you don't know what it's like inside me. How do I leap over that wall? How do I have a significant conversation with another consciousness? How do I feel human *and* unalone?

It didn't occur to me that I was lonely until I read Plato's *Apology* and suddenly I wasn't: someone was finally talking to me how I wanted to be talked to.

The *Apology* has one of the few plots that interests me. Socrates martyrs himself for his consciousness. Consciousness—the only subject that always interests me. Stories are stories because of what they say not because of what happened.

Adam was bored alone, then Adam and Eve were bored together. Said Kierkegaard. Said Markson.

"*In summa*: my lonesomeness is now a twosomeness."

We read in solitude,
To escape solitude.

III

"Imagination—that's god's gift to make the act of self-examination bearable."

Novels and poems and essays are lies and tricks and deceits—bless them.

"Only an artist understands that he or she is condemned to be free, and understands that it means . . . to live in solitude."

"It doesn't seem possible to be an artist and not be sick."

"There are many ways to make a living. Most of them are failures."

A writer is someone who makes a living (or doesn't) out of being human.

Why I get lonely in groups and have to retreat to books: writers—good ones—risk getting to the point.

Reading a good book is like getting drunk and not having to worry about a hangover.

When the author you love hangs himself, a part of yourself is lost. You venture out into the world not just sad but alone—who will I turn to for help when I can't make sense of the world I find myself in?

An author's death is a reminder that I only ever had myself to turn to, which is no turning at all—or is just a turning in circles.

The only way to leave a party is a long walk home.

"Thinking with someone else's brain, Schopenhauer called reading."

All writing asserts: I'm in here.
All reading: me too.

IN VIVO

Life can only be understood backwards;
but it must be lived forwards.
—-Kierkegaard

CONTENTS

CHAPTER 1: CONCEIVING THE PROJECT
[October 4, 2013 - October 10, 2013]

Everyone knows memoir is about the past.

But what if it's not? What if on page one of a memoir the author had no more idea where the work was headed than the reader did? This is not idle wonder. I ask because this is the case at hand: the author of this memoir does not know where this is headed. Not exactly.

I know that for this to be--or rather *become*--a memoir events will have to occur such that I undergo a change from who I am now to who I will be by the end of the book. That's why memoir is about the past. The narrating subject utilizes the tools of *memory* to access an earlier version of the self and locate/ describe/articulate a change from that self to some later one, often the one sitting there writing for you.

The problems of memory are legion and well known to memoir readers, yet they are not the memoirist's problems alone but problems that belong to any experiencing subject awash in time and perpetual change. How did *I* come from *him*? With that question begins a story. If we answer in writing we call it a memoir. When we answer in our private minds we call it a self.

It is the responsibility, therefore, of the person--not just the memoirist--to make sense of the past, to make meaning from it. Our very selves depend on the process. And I can trust therefore that the self who looks back from the end of this book will be other than the one who sets out here, if only slightly. This is a journey, then, and a journey is most honest when we do not know the destination. I trust that by the end of this book I will know what the book is about. The experiment will reveal, not just produce, the results. Though if I'm to offer a hypothesis now it's that the result will be a self that remains a work in progress. If that is too uncontroversial to need confirming, let me add that while that project normally occurs in hindsight, what's to stop it from occurring moment to moment--or at least chapter to chapter? And that no memoir is finally written, at least not while the author lives. Aristotle thought we must wait fifty years after a person's death to know whether they lived happily. The final revisions are not even ours--but our followers'--to make.

Not much consciousness is required before we begin to invent and reinvent ourselves. When we become self-conscious of this process it's a quick jump to wondering how loosely our stories need to be tied to the events of our lives and what follows from degrees of uncoupling--uncommon self-awareness or mental illness or what in between?

Another question we might ask is what of the future self? I am certain that a future me will look back at the me typing these words and see me as grist for the mill of his eventual self.[*] His larger and more inclusive self, by necessity. The future this way can leave the present feeling very small. Am I by this logic always less than I will be? I say no. Is the acorn less than the tree? Sitting here--at Denny's, it turns out, with the place mostly to myself--I feel complete in my existence, as I always have. And yet I know that when I look back from a later completeness that if not *more* will nevertheless be *other*. And so my interest here: to flip memoir inside out and write that

---

[*] Revising this on June 2, 2014, I now confirm this is the case.

change of self before and as it occurs. A memoir, that is, not of the past but of the present and of the future.

I could execute this approach for any period of life and over any scale of time. Even by the time I leave Denny's something in me will have changed, if only I can identify and represent it in language. But it is not merely as an experiment with the continuity of self that I want to take up this project. I'd like for the stakes to be more than academic, and so here I admit the proximate cause for my writing this book: I find myself at the time of this writing in my final year of graduate school in need of a creative nonfiction thesis. The thesis I've been working on up till now, a collection of essays having to do with Oregon, is fine and well, but as inevitably happens I've lost interest in it. I've allowed that project to squeeze me into a box that doesn't fit me--or at least doesn't fit me well yet.

The specifics of that would bore you. They bore me. That's part of the problem. So we'll skip them. Suffice it to say, this is an escape: from that project, from this self.

Writing about the process of writing my thesis *as my thesis* allows me the additional pleasure of problematizing another of memoir's standard tropes. A memoir always promises its own becoming (and often accounts for it as well), but this one, by tracking that becoming, cannot be assured, except abstractly, of that eventuality. Meaning: I might die or be otherwise waylaid from completion.*

Before going any further, it seems necessary at this point to establish some guidelines for myself. To maintain my limitation to the present, I'll write this book in dated sections. Within a section I will provide backstory as necessary, but

---

* From writing, sure, but also from living the "story."

the subject matter will be limited to the present. At no point during composition will my narrator have access to future events.

I hear your concern (that is, I project one of my concerns) that this is an idea born of a desire to avoid any "real work." There's some truth to this. I've never been interested in--which is probably to say I've never been good at--inventing material. I've always been more interested in thinking about what's at hand. And I'm not much interested in plot. Things happen, things happen--all I want to know is how they're experienced.

Another objection I have to this project already is that it risks becoming "just" a journal rather than a memoir. If I don't pull a proper narrative out of these pages, that's how it's likely to end up. But this is a risk I don't see how to avoid and am willing to take.

My strongest objection might be that this is some meta game that plays with the memoir form only because it can. To what end, I ask myself, am I setting out to write this book? To render the experience of becoming from the inside, I say as sincerely as I can. My friend B. (about whom more below, I'm sure) recently said that form is not some container in which we dump content. The two are always indistinguishable--as I hope they especially are here. The form--which is meta, a self-aware journal perhaps--allows the particular kind of story I intend to tell here: the one of how I becomes I.

I can take this further. The form here not only allows the kind of change I mean to leave an account of on the page, it even produces it. Does it not? A self-aware journal cannot naively record events without shaping them--and won't my life become, in part, a living out of the requirements of the direction this work takes? My sense is of course it will. Yet it occurs to me that here is an example of memoir being nearly indistinguishable from self. My actions are often--or at least when I'm at my most conscious--guided by an understanding of who I am and how this aligns with who I want to be. What's added here is but a record and possibly an enhanced degree of self-scrutiny.

Back at the apartment, I find S. playing with M., our cat. S. peeks around the corner, where M. is crouched and ready to attack. At the sight of S., she leaps up and drags her claws down the wall. We are proud like parents of how M. can leap and we do not expect to have our pet deposit returned when we move out of our apartment next June.

I tell S. I've had an idea that might be fun to pursue in lieu of my Oregon essays and explain the current project. She knows the difficulty I'm having with the essays and responds by saying, "in vivo," which I do not know as an expression but sounds to me like it must mean "in the living." I say that might work as a title and make my working title the subtitle.*

The idea of the forward-facing memoir did not come to me one day *ex nihilo*. To my experience, the way an idea crystallizes is more like this: years of reading, thinking, processing a proto-idea, working it periodically to see if it will take form, failing at this. When it won't coalesce, you-- meaning *I*--put it back in the subconscious and wait for time to ready the material. Periodically you check back and though the material is different, more malleable, it's not yet ready, and you wait. This goes on for some time until eventually when you're thinking about other subjects, other problems, it returns to you. You push on it a little just because and suddenly something shifts and there before you is not the thing you had been trying to force into existence but that thing's cous-

---

* The title turned subtitle turned no title was *Here Now*.

in. A form presents itself and the task you assign yourself is to actualize it. It's a discovery as much as an invention and creativity will come in the arrangement of what you've been sitting on for some time. An upshot is that now that things are beginning to settle you can really go after them. I've found what I didn't know I was looking for and now I'm off and running. Running at it with a full pot of coffee at my beckon. I'm back at Denny's (the chronology's all mixed up here now).

I'm writing this late at night in a lonely diner so that I might get lost in it. That kind of artistic romance appeals to me. Part of me thinks if I can work myself into a caffeinated delirium I might achieve a kind of freedom and out of which I'll surprise myself. Fond memories are returning to me of nights like this in college when a friend and I would go to a diner to pursue mayhem in the form coffee, American Spirits, and fiction writing about the nature of no-self. We were looking desperately for something and though my something was not his something the fact that we were both looking and that we were both desperate was enough and so we were allies, co-conspirators in this life. We stayed up all night, crazy mad Buddhists. The texts we were writing, like all the texts we read, like the unwritten texts of futures, were spiritual texts . . .

Consider this backstory so you understand the kind of person I am, why I'm at Denny's this night, and what it is I'm still looking for.

Those Buddhist nights were as close as I ever got--and I can't help but think the closest anyone from my generation ever got--to a proper scene. We walked home at sunrise and we were more than just young. The generation before mine remembers the sixties, the era some of us still steer by. We got no sixties of our own, but we were there at the tail end of that memory. And so we built from what remained: from conversations, little snippets of things, borrowed ideas, influences, the stuff we pick up off the ground.

CHAPTER 2: FREE WILL
[OCTOBER 11, 2013 - OCTOBER 17, 2013]

Just now, F. texted, E. texted, and B. called. All
to say that V. has checked into the hospital, her
contractions now minutes apart. How many minutes
seems to depend on who you talk to or maybe who's
counting. But this fact is consistent among the
sources: the baby (known affectionately as the
Bean) will arrive soon. Only B. noted that tonight
is a full moon.
    I like to think that we're all attuned to the
sky this night. I intend to stay up late into the
dark night getting these words down. It's comfort-
ing to think of my close friends also out there
entering their own mysteries. F., B., and I say
maybe we'll meet up later to drink coffee somewhere and wait for word from E.
    The three of us and V. met just over two years
ago when the program started, the four Creative
Nonfiction students in our cohort. The three of
them agreed to be roommates before meeting-- and
stayed roommates till V. and E. moved into a place
together. The four of us bonded that first year as
desperate people sometimes do. I was unsure of my
decision to be in the program at all. If I was a
real writer, some Hemingway side of me accused, I
wouldn't need this support. A more sensible side
of me--the side that had been working a factory for
shit wages and hadn't had health insurance for two
years--said support's just what I needed. And so I
was there, better off financially than I'd been in
a while, but even so wondering if it was worth it.
I clung to those three as they clung to me.

Wait, these predictions come too easy. F. has texted again. V. is being sent home. Not ready just yet, say the professionals. And how would V. know, first pregnancy? The due date was October 15. The same night that Katherine Boo was on campus to give the fall's Big Deal lecture. I assigned her book, *Behind the Beautiful Forevers*, to my students and finally read it myself. V. had been telling me to do so since it was published. Boo's writing is an important model for V.'s work and we all thought it was serendipitous the two dates aligned, as long as the Bean didn't arrive on time.

After Boo's talk, F.'s boyfriend, J., a fiction writer, said that he'd never felt a stronger urge to write nonfiction. Strangely, since the talk I've been having an urge to write fiction, something I've done almost never. I find it strange-- though familiar, how familiar--how readily the mind wants to flee from one thing to the next. Why this sudden interest in fiction?

By the conventions of language--and therefore of "reason"--I *have* urges, but this urge feels like it *has* me. Where did it come from? Why has it settled here? And how do I make it go away?

The so-called problem of free will has confounded philosophers since time immemorial. Are we agents or effects of change? Free or determined? Our civilization is based on an assumed agency and the moral responsibility this allows. But the question is always begged: if we choose our behavior, how do we choose how to choose, and how do we choose how to choose how to choose? You see where this ends up. Reason at this point sides with all scientific evidence that we behave first and trick ourselves into thinking it was a choice after.

Over the years as I've seen the lingering influence of the past in an infinite series of new presents, I've come to believe more than anything in luck. Metaphysically, it's the only thing that holds up to any scrutiny. Is this a nihilistic position? I don't think so. Meaning is something I live with, as I find it, receive it, and sometimes produce it. It's the orienting lens through which I'm always trying to look. The fact that I can't account for why meaning means so much to me does not in itself bother me. If the self is to my best intelligence unreal the world does not vanish.

And yet many I know not only don't believe in luck, they are offended by the thought of it; they believe in God or themselves--and though these each have psychological reassurances to recommend them, I feel assured in my position by the facts themselves: had I had their experiences, I too would choose God or myself. How could I not? And so in the landscape of my own way of understanding I've won the meta-game. Of course, in theirs, so have they. And around we go.

Let me take a different approach and attend to what is before me. Here I am writing. How do I decide which word to write next? Much of this work seems already done for me by the syntactical patterns that have become my habit. At point no choice different me sunflowers to grow. Except to make a point. It's only in the most convenient sense of the word that I can be said to be the author of any book at all, let alone one that doesn't know where it's headed. If I won't know what this book is until it is written, it feels strange to call it mine before I can read it.

After all, it's clear that I am not the source of me. I've drawn that spiral before. It never ends. Rather, I am the product of processes that precede me and occur outside me.

Just as some confluence of causes produced the effect of Sam Harris writing, "You are not controlling the storm, and you are not lost in it. You are the storm," so too does the same confluence of causes allows you to complete this sentence for yourself and wonder privately why you completed it the way . . .

The preceding conditions that produce the events of now might be mechanistic or they might be mental/cultural (or mind and brain might be another needlessly troublesome dichotomy), but . . . *see, how quickly we catch on.*

It does matter, though, from where we watch. And when I watch I from I, I feel this watching to be a choice. But infinite regressions abound. When people who know me watch me they see predictable behavior and maybe predictable variance from same. It's only from my POV that it feels like a decision to get more coffee. These people who know me know how hard it is for me to stay up late.

S. just looked over my shoulder and said that I'm getting too abstract again. You will understand that she is not the first person to say so about my writing.

One way to get more specific is to think about the mindfulness class I dropped yesterday. S. was concerned that my transcript would look bad with a "W." Not so secretly, I'm always partway hoping to be offered an excuse to drop out, so this only enticed me a little further. In fact, though, a "W" means nothing in my world. Why did I want to drop the class in the first place? And, prior to that, why did I sign up?

I'll take these chronologically: my interest in meditation has always been inseparable from my interest in memoir—the underlying connection being the impulse to trouble the easy assumption of self. To attend to the construction of the self is to remind yourself how ghostly it is, you are, I am.

In college and the first years after, I meditated regularly, sometimes frequently. There was all sorts of metaphysical baggage attached to the practice at the time. As the metaphysics faded away, so did the practice. At the same time, I began writing more seriously. The kind of concentration required by writing seemed to scratch the itch meditation used to poke at for me. It placed my attention outside myself (even when I was writing about myself--the "I" on the page is never as subjective as the one "in your head") and thereby relieved some of its pain (in bursts, when things were going well).

But I missed meditation the way you miss old friends, and I had time in my schedule and free tuition at my disposal, so I signed up. And the dropping? Well, the class ended up being more about stress-reduction and group therapy than meditation. It was a good course but not the one I was looking for. (If the fiction thing ends up sticking, though, I'll have forgone a good opportunity to gather material.)

The instructor, Erik Storlie, was an old-school American meditator, meaning he was on the scene in the '60s. He lived in Berkeley then, got into LSD and Zen, the latter of which he helped bring back to Minnesota. His teacher, Katagiri Roshi, is someone I've been reading about for years in the work of Natalie Goldberg. Besides, Storlie and Goldberg, two other authors I admire, Robert Pirsig and Steve Hagen, were involved at the Minnesota Zen Center, where I sometimes go.

What is my point here, that it's a small world or that I feel like I missed out? Could it be that I'm not the one to ask what is the point and that we can find patterns wherever we look for them?

The rain outside is steady and for the moment I feel good about my life. This is liable to change in a given moment--my mood as well as the weather--it always does. Just yesterday, some small frustrations with the publisher of a book I'm doing on Eminem threw my whole life into perilous doubt: Why be a writer? Why work so hard? Will I ever obtain a career or sufficient income? I'm bored by such concerns, but occasionally they come, regardless of my boredom.

And now today things are good in my heart and I can't imagine how they could ever be bad. I mean, I can imagine it, hypothetically, but the possibility just seems so unlikely, the suffering so far away. It has something to do with the rain, the nighttime, M. moving like she's got the devil in her. Is it a Portland thing? A Safety thing? Comfort. Content. How can I not be in the rain? I took a walk just now and am reassured. Cocooned, held, supported, made whole. I somehow belong.

The frustrations with the Eminem book were really an opportunity or occasion to feel stress more than a cause of the stress. Frustrated or not, I'll get the book done. What's getting to me is something more ambient in these years and my desire to write this book. Probably it matters that these frustrations appeared on a Wednesday, the morning after my evening thesis class.

The thesis class is at the center of my ill-at-ease-ness, my illness at ease. The purpose of the class is for the twelve writers in my cohort to meet weekly to share our work and support one another in writing our theses. It sounds ideal. And yet something in me goes all haywire. Bracketing off my own confusions and dissatisfactions with my thesis project (and allowing that these confusions and dissatisfactions may even be a healthy part of the writing process), even bracketing off the contagious anxiety that spreads among a group of artists all trying very hard to appear casually impressive among a group of peers, I'm left with a more fundamental discomfort at being in the classroom.

With only a handful of exceptions from a lifetime of schooling, I have always hated being in a classroom. Nothing makes me feel more inadequate as a human being than entering a classroom. My intelligence and articulateness leave me alone with my insecurity. Why this happens can best be explained by remembering that it always has, which proves reason enough for it to continue. Exceptions are always more telling than norms, and since I've had more years than I'd like to reflect on this I have connected a few dots to reveal this pattern: those class in which I've felt comfortable are those in which I've felt nurtured and challenged rather than judged.

The common thing is the atmosphere. And when I teach, it's a nurturing atmosphere that I try to cultivate before I think about any actual "teaching." I don't, by the way, dislike entering a classroom as a teacher. And to the best of my self-knowledge this isn't a matter of my relationship with authority. Being an authority is the thing I like least about teaching. It feels so fraudulent. I try to meet my students first as someone who can relate to their situations and only second as someone who's a little further along and might have some advice to offer. I know what it's like to care passionately about education and yet remain a mediocre (or worse) student. That's a suitable description of me to this day. I know what it's like to want to like school (the idea of it sounds so pure) and fail to do so (never lives up, rarely lives up).

It could be because I teach creative writing, but so many of the students I see are just barely hanging on (maybe the--who, geography students (?)--are models of mental health). Maybe it's because I feel like I know what they're dealing with and because I know that it's possible to find exceptions that I try to be one. I see them in need of connection and I try to offer it.

Does this sound like stress and like maybe I shouldn't have dropped that meditation class after all? No, it was the right decision. (I try to live as though all decisions made were made correctly.) Even a meditation class is sometimes a class. It matters how we choose to understand things. And we make choices even if we don't know why we make the ones we do.

I chose my collection of Oregon essays to turn in to my thesis class and now it's time to finish them. A draft is due Tuesday for my readers: in addition to V., B., and F., the professor and two other students. They will have one week to read the manuscript before we meet the following week to discuss. Over the same week, I'll be reading someone else's poetry manuscript. Later in the semester I'll read theses by V., B., and F.

V.'s book is an ethnobiographical narrative/ memoir of her time living with the Tarahumara in and around Chihuahua City, when she was on a Fulbright. B. is working in lyric and drawing to essay bees. F., unsatisfied with her attempts to write memoir, abandoned nonfiction last year for the creative license of fiction. She's working on a story collection exploring the Argentinian diaspora. I am proud of the work they're doing and am eager to read their manuscripts. But I'm up first and there isn't enough of this book yet to switch, so I will work this week on finishing up drafts of those essays and hoping that in so doing my interest in them is rekindled.

CHAPTER 3: OUR DINNER WITH THE GIANT
[OCTOBER 18, 2013 - OCTOBER 24, 2013]

I woke up on the 18th just a little before F. called
to say V. was in the hospital and what should we
do. It was early and she and B. had dropped V. and
E. off earlier still. They should sleep is what we
decided, while I read. It was Friday, after all.
No school, etc. We arranged to meet up later for
breakfast and baby talk. High Times Cafe, where I
want to stay up all night romantically, heroical-
ly composing and growing a Russian beard, clothes
of material. Fibers. Next time or the time after
I'll go there to write on this project. This stuff
should be written proximate danger or at least bo-
hemia. The cafe is vegan, or mostly. They're open
all night, or mostly. They have history, lots of
it. I could go there and go crazy and disappear and
turn into a radical and wake up in the morning in
padded slippers and cotton pajamas in the suburbs.
Time goes on one way there while other dimensions
pile up comforts. You'll want to enter all dimensions, all the ones you have access to. This is
the access point.
    We have identified this point this morning.
The coffee is strong and my nerves are already
rattling. The pulses wavering here started back
in some darkness. In darkness, to light, it is
bright out today. We eat breakfast and note sym-
bolically that the baby has chosen the right day
to appear. This much is clear. We pay cash. They
take only cash. It's that kind of place, you see.
This is how I speak of romance. We pay cash and
we go to the car, F.'s. We drive around the block.

Again, I disappear. I reappear in the back seat.
An indeterminate amount of time has passed. We
are across the street, parking. We walk to the
hospital. There are giraffes and children but no
babies in the lobby. Now F. disappears as B. and
I grapple with the future and all about it. All
about it. Madness. The kinetic kind. To be a writer, to be an artist, to make, to give birth, to do
so in a . . . with a . . . among . . . together,
some of us, going somewhere. I'd like to be more
specific. We'd like to be more specific. We do not
know. It makes so much more sense looking back.
When we met, when we didn't know what we were getting into, when we got ourselves through it. Now
we're through, or close enough. There's the final
push: our theses must be finished. But the end is
in sight. And then what comes next? Life. B. has
received an offer to have her own farm in Maine,
but she doesn't feel done here. I have no plans
but, today this day as on some days, pockets full
of hope. V. is upstairs at some stage in delivery.
We wait. F. returns. She knows the giraffes well
and has focus, which she demonstrates by bringing
water.

There is nowhere to hide at the noon hour.

These labors can feel interminable. There is
nothing for us to do here. We go. I go running
with my cell phone in my hand like people I judge
cruelly in case this time someone calls. B. goes
to a friend in need. F. has her own business to
attend to, which is my way of saying I don't know
where she has gone. I call her after my run to
find out and we decide to have dinner. You don't
need to know everything, so we'll jump ahead to
about five o'clock and dinner, Indian. There is
F., there is J., there is me. A little later,
there is B. coming from seeing her friend. There
is palak paneer, there is something with peas,
there is nan but not enough nan. Time passes and
finally there is more nan. There is a text message.

There is a baby! We four pile into the car and drive a few blocks down the street until: There is S. She gets in. The five of us drive, we drive. Not far and there we are at the hospital with the giraffes. There are so many giraffes. We proceed through a normal routine of routines: an elevator, asking for directions, etc. There is a security check in and no one but me has ID, so they must be processed with a processing camera. They are insane. We are wild. We are not safe. We mean well, but god help us. No we are fine, but we are giddy from baby. S. takes her processing photo and everyone thinks she's special meaning retarded meaning no offense but that's what it looks like. She's never been good in front of a camera, all her beauty evaporates in her self-protection, but this is the first time she's leaned in just so her forehead booms and her teeth expand in all the wrong directions. And that's not even to get started with the other fisheye-lens happenings. Since I have my ID my security card features my driver's license photo, which looks like a criminal who might be a distant cousin of me: brown hair and and and . . .

. . . inside the door, V. is readying herself, her baby is twenty minutes old. F. and B. go in. J., S., and I wait in the hall. A minute later we are invited and there is E. practicing swaddling. There is V., and there is A.! He looks content. And his mother is glowing, as she has glowed since conception. Not A.'s as much as her own. V. glows. Present tense. She goes on glowing as sandwiches are retrieved via a computer portal that wastes just piles of valuable time, so valuable, so much so soon. And glowing glowing the night.

Tomorrow we bring donuts and a balloon and everyone wants the ones with icing. I hold A. in my arms. He wiggles. I am steady.

Tomorrow again and tomorrow again. A week later it's tomorrow again. A month later, who knows. You can bet.

CHAPTER 4: CHANGE OF CHANGE OF PLANS
[OCTOBER 19, 2013 - OCTOBER 31, 2013]

Wait wait wait. Hold up! Damned if I can't not get
out of this box. Ever since I turned in that manuscript to my readers I've felt like it's not such
a bad project after all. I won't switch, I can't.
I think I've done good work there. Has good work
not been done?

   There are other reasons too, reasons anti. S.
made a damning point about in vivo: how is that
different from a blog? I told her, "It's totally
different from a blog." I said it with great authority and literary condescension. Then I started
laughing. I had invented the blog! Independently,
I had invented the blog. But it's not a blog, see,
because I'm going to save it up, put it on paper,
and release it to the world all at once. A blog
not in real time but in publishing time: typing,
revising (will revising be allowed?*), editing,
submitting, getting rejected, trying again, trying again ad infinitum, being accepted, being published in a future so far removed from the events
that this won't be a blog or a memoir but straight
history. Archives. Blog or not, though, in the
moment, what is this book? What is it to the me
sitting here writing it? (I am at this now writing
moment at Common Roots cafe. It is Halloween. F.
and B. are across the table from me. I am drinking
Indeed's fresh hop pale ale and don't know it's
name.† The week has been odd. But I won't stick

----

* Yes, in the minor sort of way described in Chapter 24.
[6/2/14]
† Mosaic Fresh Hop American Ale. [6/2/14]

such oddness in parentheses.) I changed, or wanted to change, my thesis for a couple of reasons.
There is the box I don't fit in. The Oregon nature
writer/charming essayist box that I admire but
feel inadequate for. You will feel inadequate. You
will continue but you will feel inadequate. And so
the box squeezes me and I want to break loose. I
am stubborn, and I like to frustrate expectations.
In many years, little has changed.

There's more. Thesis class, important class,
the one where we finally get to share the works we
have been working on and get feedback and encour-
agement on more than just a little snippet. Part
of the class involves a presentation. I was in the
first group of presenters and here's how my presentation went: disastrously bad. Disastrously. Almost from the beginning I broke into a sweat so bad
my glasses were sliding off my nose, which caused
me to get nervous and forget what I was trying to
say, which caused me to sweat more, which caused
total mental shutdown. I mumbled and stumbled and
stuttered until they let me leave.[*] It's much easier for me to talk about memoir than it is for me
to talk about whatever this Oregon thing is, so
part of wanting to switch is the thought of my final
presentation . . . See, I'm interested in memoir
and one thing this book allows me to do is think
about it. If I were to give a "craft talk" on this
book I'd talk about how this is like other memoirs
that are only just removed from their subject (*The
Year of Magical Thinking* comes to mind, so does
A *Heartbreaking Work of Staggering Genius*); I'd
talk about how it's like those books where someone
goes out to do something and document it (Thoreau
and too many weird contemporary examples to bother
naming). What I'd say makes this book different

---

[*] F. claims I "did great" in this presentation, which either
suggests that she is far too kind to ever be trusted or confirms everything about the subjective nature of perception.

is it tries to do both at once. One challenge I'd face is that grad school is on its surface way less interesting than almost anything else someone might do for the sake of the book. I'll have to trust you, reader, to see that as in all memoir the subject matter is merely the occasion for the real story, which is the self in time. I'll say how all memoirs account for their own coming into being, this one just makes it more explicit.

OK but so that's what I'm not doing anymore, not switching to that, sticking with the previous, not to say original, plan. Why. Yes why. Putting it together I said to myself, Hey this here is a book you've written. I don't remember writing it, but nevertheless here it is. It's no small thing to have made something. And wait there's more. I workshopped with my group of readers (minus V.). They gave me lots to think about it and it's think-ing I want to do. Make it more better. I'm on a good cloud the day this happens. But wait again there's more still.

The same day there's an official event put on by the department. To relate this event I will switch to fiction, but first let me explain the decision to give it to you in fiction. There was a before, a during, and an after the event. B. attended the first two, I attended the latter two. The next night, B. and I drove over to St. Paul to attend another literary event. In the car on the way there I told her about how it was at the "after" and she told me how it was at the "before." Suffice it to say, how in each case was considered to be bad. It was then I felt that dangerous and devil-ish impulse to expose to reveal to take revenge. There's just no excuse for that kind of . . . But I've been mean in print before and it doesn't do no good for nobody in the end--or not enough any-way. And since I'm switching from switching why don't I write an MFA novel? Memoir is best served when its author isn't. I've never written fiction.

It's a wacky fucking idea, but I kinda am drawn to
it. There will be characters based on characters,
scenes based on scenes, themes based on experience.

CHAPTER 5: THE MFA NOVEL
[FICTIONAL PRESENT OR WHATEVER HAPPENED TO NOVEMBER?]

I can't bear the thought that this will lead nowhere. I don't care where, but somewhere. And but
what is this but a fear of nonexistence that I
wasn't aware belonged to me (I wasn't aware I belonged to)?

A fear of nonexistence is a failure to trust
in the present moment. It is to make the present
dependent for its meaning its value upon the future. It is to fail to stop believing in god, to
be brave enough to really let go. Let go. How could
we live if we did not always hold ourselves back?
Nonexistence is our history, our destiny, and if
we're honest our reality. We are not honest. I am
not honest. I want to be honest enough to be the
god I don't believe in. To be the god I do believe
in. And yet but so gods live in cages as big as
imagination.

In the present moment, what am I scared of?
I ask myself so that I might answer myself. I'm
scared that if this doesn't lead somewhere it's
without value, and because *it* is *I*, the syllogism
tells me that I am without value. I am worthless.
Intellectually, I wouldn't defend that position,
but emotionally there's part of me that cannot
escape it. And so I am ashamed, not of who I am
but that I am. This much of me is with Silenus: I
wish I didn't exist. Next best option: cease to.
Exhibit A: self-starvation. Exhibit B: avoidance
of attention. Exhibit C:

SCENE:

I have to stop. I can't go on with it. There's no way short of parable the fiction won't be read as straight *roman a clef*. I can't have it both ways and make this public without taking responsibility.

Let me take another approach. If a student turned something like this chapter in to workshop I would encourage him (it would be a him) to localize the abstraction for the reader. Can the ideas fit into a story? Can the quest itself be dramatized? Either that or talk to your therapist. (Because I teach nonfiction, though, he will respond: this is my therapy. And I will say: I've taught you well. Not really. Sort of. I'm not supposed to say that. My students are in pain. Given that I teach nonfiction, this hints of tautology, but there it is: a classroom full of young people who have known and continue to know suffering. Thank god for them. We are all struggling so hard to hold on. I want to tell my students that I feel them, that there are many of us out there, out here, who feel them, that they are felt, that it's not that bad. Because it's true, it's not that bad, except when it is. It is.)

How are my mixed feelings about the program about me and not about the program? That's a story I could write without complaint. Allow me to meet some narrative expectations. The rest we'll get to in due time. (Oh my god, what did happen to November?!)

I finished a draft of my thesis and turned it in to workshop. I got good feedback that I was ready to apply to the manuscript but promptly stopped thinking about that project. I met with a professor who offered to read the full manuscript in January and help me get it to a press I like. This was very exciting. Again, I promptly forgot about the project. There were easier things to lose sleep over. Like what's next? The benefit of this program is that it has spared me that question for a few years, which is to say I've been sleeping better than before the program. Should I teach? Do I need to get a job? Am I a total failure? Yes, I'm a total failure. I sent out resumes. Help! One press says it plans to use me as a contractor. That should buy an occasional night's sleep.

Then my mom's cousin died. One of my cousins and one of her daughters came to stay with us and go to the funeral. I inherited his snow boots and they are good snow boots and now my feet aren't so cold. As much as I liked having cold wet feet, it is better sometimes to have warm dry feet. This is how good things are made even better. He was a Christian in the unusual sense that he always met a person with compassion. You suffer and he suffered along with you, asking for nothing. Needless to say, as suffering is unbounded, these shoes are unfillable.

in here releases and I think I must finish in vivo. And then what--in there; in()action; in due time; in your face; inevitably; in progress? Everything is artifice.

My sister comes to visit. She is quitting her

job. She is travelling the world. She is changing her career. She will not be stopped by the likes of you. She teaches us something. She leaves.

CHAPTER 6: STUDIES IN BLUE
[NOVEMBER 27, 2013 - NOVEMBER 30, 2013]

1.

2.

3.

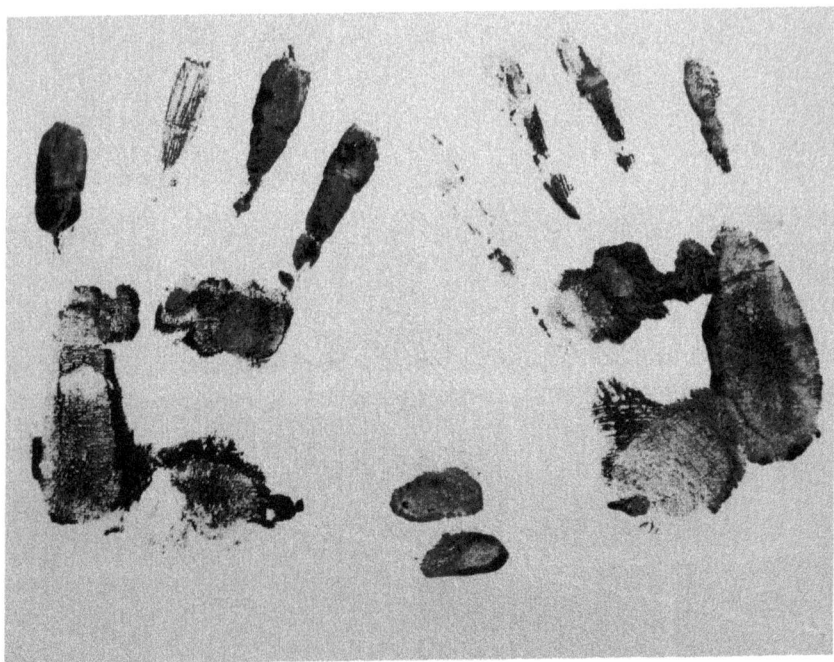

4.

5.

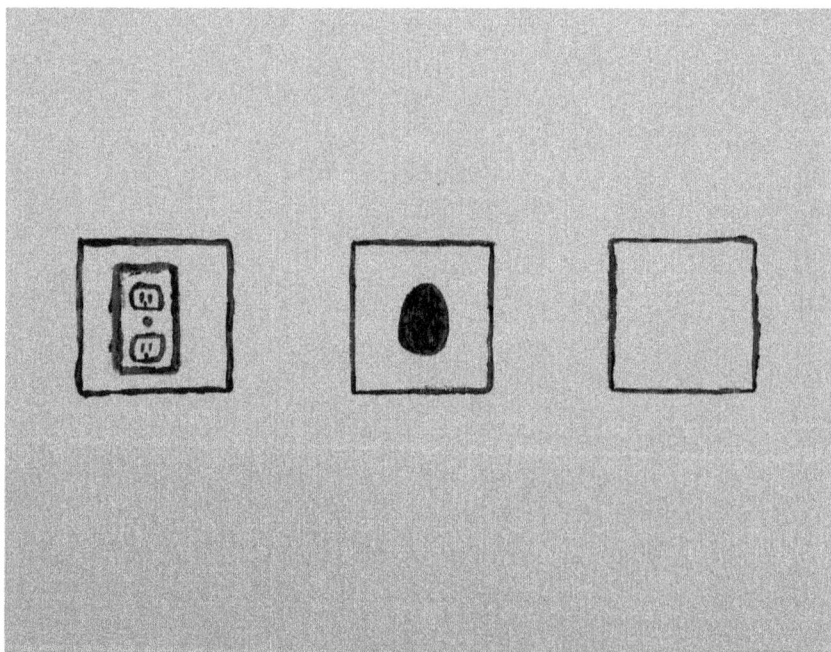

6.

Suppose I were to begin by saying that I had fallen in
with a color. Suppose I were to speak this as though
... Suppose I shredded my napkin as we ...
... an affinity I bear...
... his for appreciation, an affinity I bear.
... love with a color ... Then I looking into an
... in this case the color ... their brown eyes ...
get from candor, or from ... are so
... a spell I brought the sky ...
want cooler ... ...
been personal.

Cleverness is so eminently one of the character...
that often it even passes for truth—

Why else ... are the details? Clearly I am
... the possibly I am a fool
persons ...

... as well as not, if objects had the color the
say.— Well, it is as you please. But what
look like is not otherwise ...

As if we could ... the color of the iris and still see

For starters, words do not look like the things then ...
(Maurice Merleau-Ponty, def poet)

Does the world look bluer from blue eyes? Probably not,
but I choose to think so (self-aggrandizement).

Mostly I have felt myself becoming a servant of sureness.
I am still looking for the brand that.

I feel confident enough of the specificity
of my relation to it to share.

It calms me to think of blue as the color of death.

For those who no mind, it is not mine, mine have a ...
any wisdom, the in beautiful, and stupid, what the ...
philosopher and Shakespeare have meant I think that ...

7.

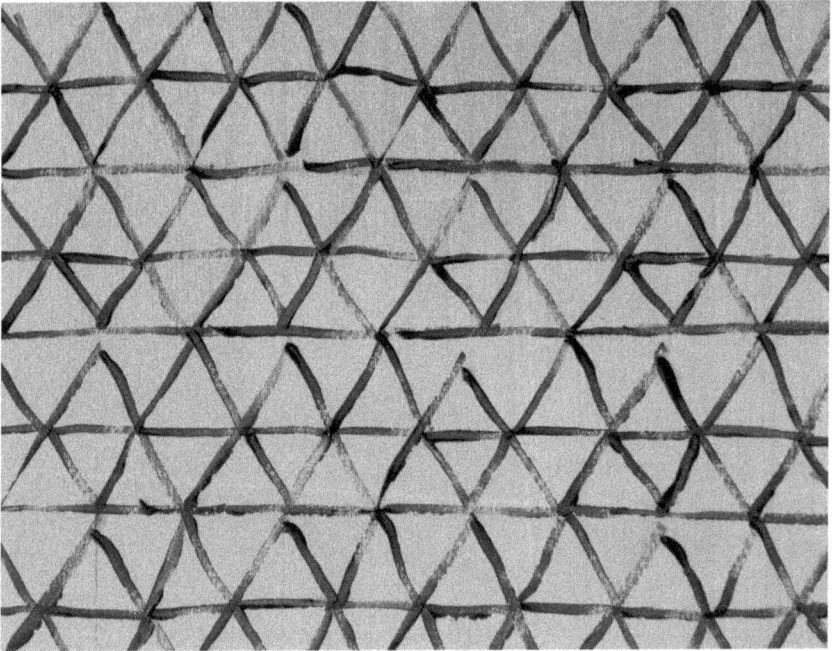

8.

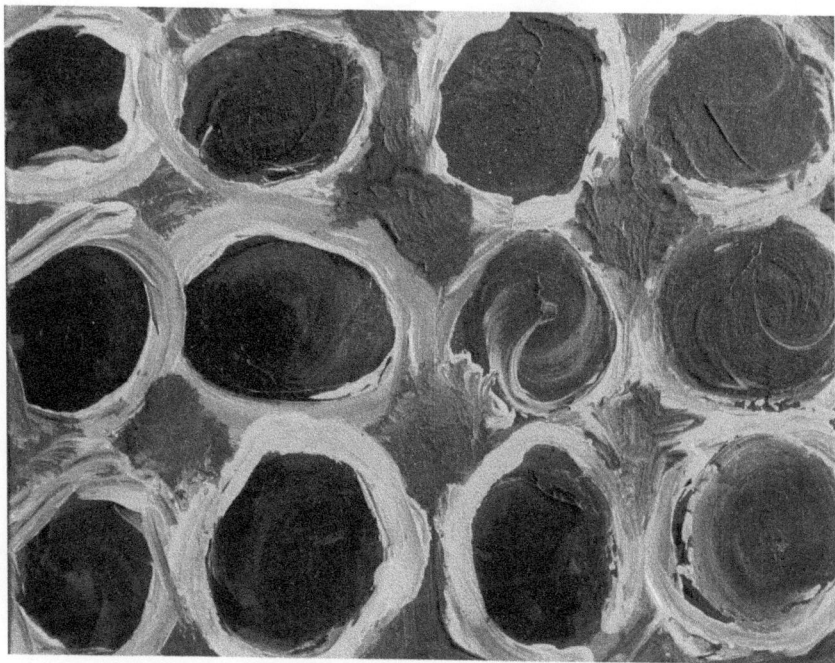

9.

in vivo

10.

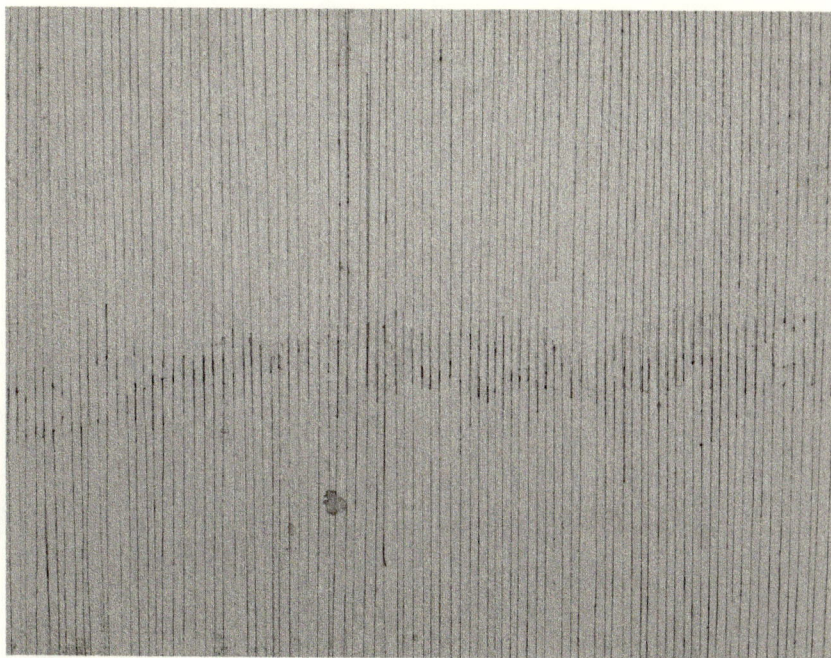

11.

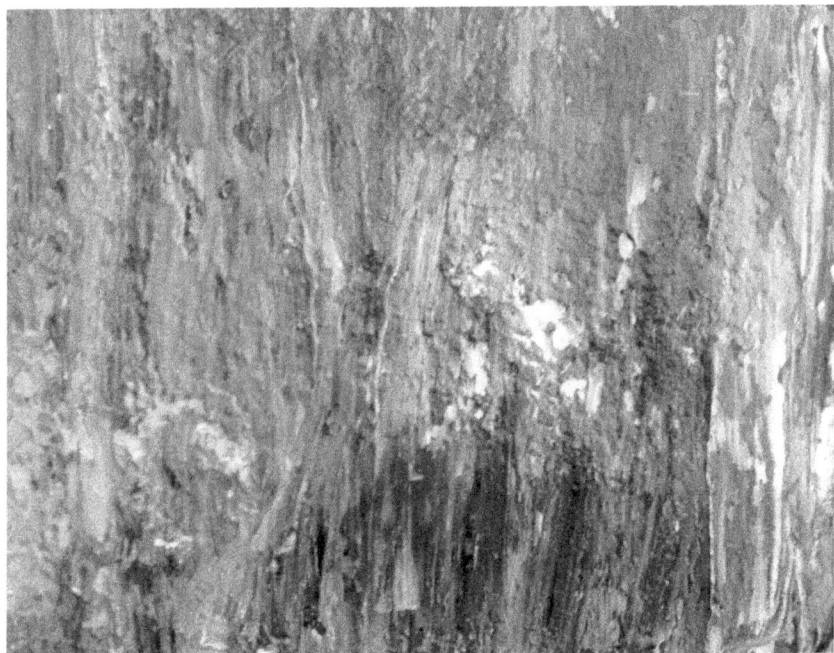

The blue could go on. The blue is quite capable.
It can hold you. You can become lost in it. If you
enter it . . . But the blue is interrupted. Interrupted by a force that waits for no color.

It is important to know what it is like.
It is like this:
It is like your nervous system is an electrical
  system.
Which it may be.
It is like your whole body has just orgasmed.
But without pleasure.
What you really are is sensitive.
And vulnerable.
Experience dropping away in icicle chunks.
Light. Gone.
Language. Gone.
What remains is red.
Symbolic red: blood, passion, rage.
One must seek the cool calm of blue.
But for the fumes of blue have produced this state.
It is like being high.
But again without much pleasure.
And not enough fear.
The red thing is coming for what's left of when the
  important chunks have fallen away.
I'm making this as clear as I can before I fall
  away.
I go to a dark quiet place to flee this red.
But this red is inside of me, taking me over.
I prostrate myself before nothingness.
I lie humbled.
Everything is outside my control.
It is all so fragile.
I lie humbled.
I lie.
I lie.

Eventually I go on lying until I am ready to move
  gently. And with gratitude.

Trying to maintain an even keel.
Tomorrow there is nothing.
I can't go on. I must go on. And so on.
And so on.

CHAPTER 7: THE CYCLE CONTINUES
[Time Immemorial - December 5, 2013]

In the name of self-knowledge I must interrogate these moods. Their intensity. Their periodicity. The breaks are steady and even. A composite week is this:

Monday--go to campus with S.; spend day in library doing work, reading, feeling productive; break for yoga; return to work; spirits high.

Tuesday--get to campus early, alone in student offices, prep to teach; teach my wonderful class, think to self teaching might be a rather good career; eat a tofu sandwich; prepare for thesis class; arrive at thesis class, spend 2-3 hours relearning how to feel ashamed of myself[*]; go to bar with Aldrich Family[†] and try to be positive (or go

---

[*] Why is this? I can't really understand it let alone adequately explain it. But something about the environment corrodes my soul. And I don't think I'm alone in this. Now why? This is not a way I'm accustomed to feeling as a writer. I didn't feel this way in previous writing classes. And I didn't feel this way in the class the visiting professor taught last spring. But I have felt this way in most other classroom settings I've been in. What's different? Why is this environment like school and not like a writing group? Hypotheses: 1) professors treat students with condescension (in general); 2) students feel like we're competing for anointment rather than collaborating for the sake of the art; 3) writing is treated as product not as process; 4) a culture of celebrity pervades; 5) cynicism is contagious; 6) we look for writing that "works" and not for writing that sets our hearts on fire; 7) writers are an insecure bunch and without a nurturing environment our insecurities cultivate themselves. But that's why I hate myself when I'm at school: I'm meant to. And because I'm prone to (another time, another place), I do so with vigor.

[†] Some combination of V., B., F., E., J., S., and me.

home and start working on recuperating emotionally).

Wednesday--stay home, recovering from thesis
hangover, trying to get swagger back; by mid- to
late afternoon life is starting to go my way again
and I can't imagine how anything could ever get
to me.

Thursday--get to campus early, alone in student
offices, prep to teach; teach my wonderful class,
think to self teaching might be a rather good career; go read; meet F. for beers and writing (and/
or work on in vivo on my own).

Friday--happy work day, whole future ahead of
me; life is grand.

Saturday--less work, but mostly ditto.

Sunday--ditto.

It's not a bad a schedule when I write it out.
(It's not even a bad schedule when I don't write
it out.) My responsibilities are few. My rewards
are many. And yet my Tuesdays flatten me and I put
myself to sleep at night by promising myself that
I can drop out as soon as I really need to. Whenever I speak this fantasy out loud, S. gets frustrated and speaks with all manner of practicality
about things that don't matter to me, things like
credentials and accomplishment. The reason not to
drop out, by my thinking, is so as not to abandon
my friends. Plus hold on to health insurance a few
more months.

Sampson Starkweather says, "Time defied by a
cartwheel." I think he is right, but only if time
is a line. If time is a circle, it might be defied by a vault. Similarly, it's only if life is a
time that it is disrupted by events. If life is a
present, then it is literally a gift and we should
be grateful. We show gratitude through love. And
because today is a Thursday, I have it to share.

CHAPTER 8: WHAT THIS BOOK IS ABOUT: A GUESS
[December 6, 2013 - December 12, 2013]

READING TENSE PRESENT

For so long I've been living my life in fast-forward. Or maybe it hasn't been that long. It feels like no time. But that could be due to the fast-forwarding. If I hadn't been going at 8X speed maybe I'd still be a young man. Maybe I still am a young man and it's only the tape itself that feels as if it's moving fast. Are you watching this movie?

The one I'm watching goes like this: you know the way some people have to check their phones every thirty seconds to see if they're still alive? From the time I announced (to myself only) my intention to be a writer six years ago,[*] I have been accelerating on a track toward constant publication. An hour here or there turned into hours-long stretches day after day turned into every waking moment me publishing something or working on something that will lead directly toward publication. My thoughts, my word, my time--it becomes *my self*--is only worthwhile as product. Watching a movie--or, god forbid, hanging out with people--can send me into fits of spasm. Dear god, how did it get this way? Wasn't escaping the perpetual urge toward production and efficiency and all that one of the things that first drew me to the leisurely world of the arts.

This book is about what then? How it is to live in this present and what it's like to hopefully

---

* Malaysia, 2007.

escape. I'll run with that for awhile and try to keep on my feet. I can run fast, I swear. And far. I have an accountant's mind. How much of my life can I account for? All of it. Is that a good thing, I'm not so sure, but it's a way of life, a way of hanging on for it. I'll sleep when I'm dead. It's that kind of deal. You must understand, I feel compelled to constantly justify my existence, which I can do only by pointing at something I made. All I'm ever doing is carving my name in shit. It's not oblivion I fear, it's what comes before it.

We are nothing heaping scorn on nothing. Except it doesn't feel that way.

And how it feels.

Yes, *how* it feels.

As Proust's narrator concludes by becoming ready to begin writing the book we're already reading,

As begin and being transpose,

As Knausgaard looks closely and patiently enough to find meaning amidst all banality,

As the calculus is an approximation approaching perfection of continuity . . .

. . . we aim to describe the true curve and its seductive properties rather than the most beautiful line between two points--life is a squiggle and yet we know it leads somewhere. This is an exercise in trust. The end is not given, the end is not given.

Do we direct our own lives from behind or from out in front (if at all)? I'm giving up my advantages. Memoir is a mode of writing.

But how can I not aim this project somewhere. Not to aim is not in this case to aim nowhere. There is a choice and what disrupts the mode here is that the choice has not been made (or assigned?) but is being (or will be) made. Made things, these selves, written or not.

And so what now but Life: an Envisioning? In college, a friend got drunk and carved L I F E into his forearm. That's the idea. The promise. A mandate. We are not in college anymore. We are in something much sicker. I have referred to cynicism only once in this manuscript so far--and then in a footnote. The tenor of this omission strikes me now as less than fully honest. An observation: when people are too scared to admit that they are sometimes scared (writers! who are what if not human, humans being what if not sometimes scared) they will some of them react defensively, some of these following the old sports adage that the best defense is a good offense.[*] Their fraudulence wears closer to the surface the harder they fight to conceal it. Writers need readers, best those who are generous enough to be sincerely and productively critical. Some decisions I make prove to be good decisions and others do not. My cynicism is reserved for those who squirm around to have things both ways favoring themselves. B. is very good at coming up with different ways of thinking about things, and with most things if you can think about them in the right way you can preempt disappointment. There is plenty to be thankful for. There is B. and V. and F. and so many others. And B. and I and the rest are trying hard to keep our good hearts pure for ourselves, our art, and our human commitments.

Is this a key turning point in the memoir? It's possible. This is stuff I've thought about (of course) before now, but if it hits me now as a powerful enough insight that it becomes a turning point in the direction of my life at this time[†] then maybe it is. What yet would it mean, that I make changes? Shall I? What changes shall I make, consequently? The fantasy of dropping out still

---

[*] Postscript here. Tears. Disappointment. Frustration. Disillusionment. Anger. Bitterness. Unhealthy drinking. Catharsis. Solidarity. Cynicism? Cynicism? Cynicism?

[†] That is, if later I look and decide this is the key turning point, then it will be. What I'm aware of now is: Is it?

occurs to me daily. I keep my equanimous distance
from emotional reaction to the nonsense, except
whether I like it or not this is my life. This is
literally what I'm doing with myself.

Let me Re-Envision. Let me re-envision the stars
and the river lights, the night's snowfall and tomorrow cool the syntactic
                    column
                 of the first
               eleven hundred
               ideas I had
                before my
              mother was born
             (she should know)
              cool them like
                the soupy
               water slush
                gathered
              in the walk-
                   ways
               into & out of
               this really
                   very
                  small
                  room
                   it's
                    so
                  very
                  small
      it couldn't get much smaller
              if Miles Davis
                  blew
                   it
                  from
                  his
                  horn
and the rest of the talk laugh cry of early on-
set melancholia, it's not even midnight and I've
been here my whole life or maybe more, or maybe
more. More like what I'm going to do with dreams

that won't be cooled. More like a book of poetry so fat you read its poetry with your biceps, your strained bulging biceps. Darkness still creeping in at the corners, but you've got this book of poetry, this fat fat book, and you are holding on for dear sweet life and you are not even considering letting go.

That's why we're talking about plans and visions. Because you won't let go even for a moment, even to get a better grip. The grip you have is not even adequate. It's the grip you have. There is no other. When people say, "Whoa, get a grip," they are not talking to you. As you well know. They are not. They very surely are not.

Plans and visions, re-. The kind of specificity writers are revered for. S. has one more year here for her program. Then we will go elsewhere for her internship for a year. Then we will go to another elsewhere and make it another here. While she does, I will do that. And we will grow older. And we will have a child. Or we will not. All futures are of this nature. They will either occur or they will not. What need is there for probability. There is yes and there is no and in the end there is only yes. And when enough yeses are recorded, well--I digress . . . The direction from the midpoint is always indeterminate, even when we don't realize so. This is a fact available to reason and experience alike. And when reason and experience align it's easy for one to feel good about oneself even if they align to tell you to feel bad. This, my friends, is called freedom. Friends, please treat me well. In turn, I will do my best. Think what it means to be American, the side effects of this condition. Bravery is required of us. Imagination is ultimately what we need, but in the meantime bravery--there is no alternative. Do I digress again? This time I do not think so. I think I'm right on point for once, aimed true at the facts of this life. How American of me to be looking so hard for the moment of change, to be trying so hard to produce the moment, to assume such a moment must come, even that it might. And how further American to feel viscerally the failure to produce this moment on command. To feel guilt and shame. I represent my country well. But I will not die for these confusions. For once, I'm not ashamed to be bored. Your story is boring, America, and there are a million of us out here in the night. We are out here with wet shoes, creeping closer to the fire as management cannot prevent. There is a bus coming to pick us up, destination TBA. TBA when you're least expecting it. TBA by a voice from the shadows. A black man in a hoodie who your iPhone thinks is a criminal. He might as well be a criminal. He's one of us. And we are coming for your iPhones. Download a security app and laser gun immediately, if you're scared. We are coming for your iPhones. What do I envision! My vision doesn't fit in a Kanye West rant. And you want to talk to me?

Knausgaard, I mentioned, pays real good attention. I could find a "turn" on a potato bug at the end of a long hallway. This is otherwise known as the calculus of perspective. A man lying in his bed . . . Get it, lying in his bed . . .

In all attending, the attender is changed. In all unattending, the unattender is changed. There will be, it seems, changing going on here. And not only are we changed but so too are we made.

If we choose to be gentler with our fragile souls, we may choose as well to intend our attending. And here, closely attuned, do we enjoy the opportunity to be like Buddhist monks who write prose poems with tealeaves, and if we are honest about what we do we must admit that at any given dx/dt the slope of our selves is a finite picture of what is occurring in consciousness. David Hume said he could find no "self" underlying experience.

I say, boy, do I say. Little boxes of what it's
like to put your boxes in a row.

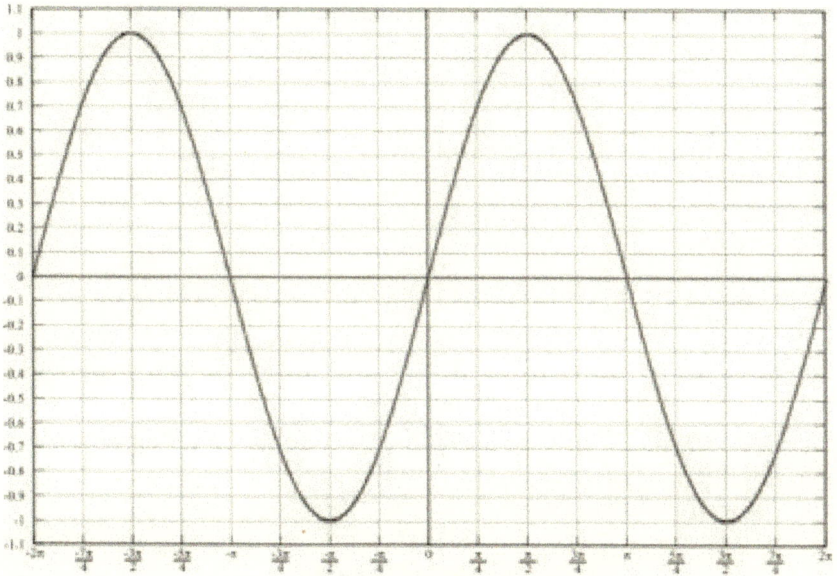

f(x)=sin of mood
f'(x)=90° out of phase with reality

On a planar surface, the z-dimension extends out
perpendicularly into the onlooker's imagination.
This is commonly known as time. This will prove
relevant later when the arrow strikes your forehead. Beware! In the meantime, be prepared to plug
in some coordinates.

At any point on the curve (x1), f'(x1) = the
slope of the slope of the slope of the slope of
the slope of the infinitesimal moment. Represented
graphically, this might be a spiral or it might
be:

gogogogogogogogogogogogogograph

The present appears asymptotic whenever you try to

represent it (no matter the medium). It resists representation because it is in which representation occurs. So what is represented (whatever the medium) must always be the representation--or media is always meta (self-referential). As is memoir. As is speech. As is redundancy.

Language as closed system, no matter how much it expands what ends up on the page is:

                    ink
                consciousness
                  language

    which if arranged properly can result in:
                communication

    which is necessarily an approximation of:
                   being

distinct from non-being insofar as metaphysics is a game we play

        a game we play

             a game we play

                  a game we play

                       a game we play

CHAPTER 9: AURAS & HANGOVERS
[December 13, 2013 - PORTLAND]

It is time to introduce K. She is an antidote to
the evil of indifference and mute hostility. What,
for example, does she do? She does this (for the
hour of now). She puts together a two- part, two-
night reading series to give the third-year students thirty minutes each in which to share their
work with a supportive and attentive audience.
Maybe that sounds to you like no big deal. This
is a test to find out whether you are us. For to
us this deal's bigness is big indeed. But let me
share my reaction: mostly dread. I want to try to
speak here to conditioning.
   My default orientation as a human being among
other human beings is to be one who sees but is
not seen. Before I was a writer I was briefly a
photographer. Somewhere along the way I internalized the feeling that it's better to be seen than
heard, and better still not to be seen either. But
the more I write, the more people keep coming up
to me and asking questions. Right to my pink face.
   Sometimes what they're asking for is for me to
read my work out loud to folks. When this is what
they're asking, I suppress my deep-down desire to
be invisible and make myself say yes. I do this
because it is the right thing to do and because I
hope that if I do it enough it will become easier
to say yes. It's not so bad, usually, anyway. As
long as I have the words there in front of me I
know more or less what to say. And if my face turns
red and if I sweat, so what, people are often more
forgiving than they're given credit for being--at

least the ones who hang out at literary events often are. And then more so strange, a time or two
I've actually enjoyed being up there in front of
other human beings asking to be looked at and considered. There's an adrenaline rush after, and a
kind of tender thrill sometimes in the living moment. I have felt that thrill in bookstores across
the Twin Cities, and the fact that this is a fact
is cause of immense relief in me. However, I have
additionally read at one MFA reading, and there I
felt the great embarrassment that is always but a
quick surprise away for me. I stood up there at
that podium and felt like my words were as inadequate and worthy of scorn as their author. I felt
judged, and what's worse: judged deservedly harsh-
ly. After, I went to my friends B. and F. to be
reassembled, only they said I was great and it was
very confusing, which is not to say more pleasant.

And so when K. asked me to read, according to
policy, I said yes and then spent the waiting
weeks praying for a snowstorm or the flu or anything that might intervene. Not only is this a
weak and shameful attitude but I admire K. deeply
and feel on top of it all guilt for wanting her
reading to disappear. Could there be more? A few
chapters back, was it clear that I was describing
a migraine? Since that last migraine and nearly
another one (somehow I dodged it) this week, I've
been a more sensitive creature than usual. I have
taken, this week, to wearing sunglasses in the
kitchen, in case any sunlight shines through the
pulled blinds. I hold my body cautiously and move
through the world slowly, prepared for attack from
light, sound, smell, motion, existence itself. You
never know where the next strike might originate.

I wake up in pain. I remain in pain. I comfort
myself through pain. I think it's a good thing I'm
not hypochondriacal. This is the kind of thing
some people would assume is a brain tumor. Whatever it is--and it's a migraine, lingering, linger-

ing--I want it gone. But we cannot vanquish from ourselves what we are. This pain is me. This fear is me.

What I want right now is to be the kind of person who can give a good reading for K.

I arrive with F. and we eat tacos and the crowd size is right and the mood is positive, and I hope that I am a contributor. This week-long migraine of a hangover is worse today than ever. My body is not mine. And what is? B. reads Virgil (yay!) and Mendel. F. reads next Lauria. With one ear I listen. With the other ear, I hear my voice to come. Then there is a break. Then the table is mine. I thank K. with a sincerity that I'm grateful to access. And the table is mine. In the three hours before now I have barely finished one beer, so scared am I of my nervous system, so disconnected are my hands from my mind. But the table is mine and I have thirty minutes. And in I dive to the words, so many words. The most words I've ever read. The best words I've ever written. I start out feeling fine, by page three I'm feeling confident, and by page nine I'm building something I've never built before. Thirty minutes in and the audience is with me. There is power, which I have figured out--for this night, now--how to allow. The transportation is so thorough that when it's over I almost expect the hangover to be gone. Almost.

This is Friday. By Saturday, finally, it is. And Monday I'm speaking to the doctor. I tell her I have migraines, she tells me I have migraines, we are great allies with respect to migraines. We discuss personality types to no final resolution. I promise not to make so many promises when the high temperature might still be below zero. I promise not to make so many promises from inside a cocoon. I promise not to make so many promises until these socks dry. I promise not make so many promises to myself.

And when I go back to Portland I forget about everything back in:

America, I'm writing to you from the rain, America.
America, the view has never been so good.
My knuckles are growing moss, America.
My paper is soaked, America, and the ink is
  running off the page
There has been a great inflation.
I can't stand my own mind either.
We are mad doggy fools, all of us seeking assur-
  ance.
America, don't spy on me, you won't like what you
  see. America, meet me in Berkeley 1956.
Our bags are packed full of grass and we're on our
  way. When this train arrives I'll still be on it.
America, tell me where the track leads.
Why won't your in-laws speak of fucking?
America, what are they so afraid of?
When will you see that astroturf is bullshit?
America, go fuck your plastic grass my erection
  isn't going anywhere. I have always been trying
  to come to the point.
America, please stop butt dialing me. I'm running
  out of minutes and I'm awaiting your call.
My sister is visiting our cousin in France and I
  don't blame her. I drink so much coffee the TV
  channels just spin.
Please, will you put those angry men to rest.
America, the Internet is calling.
America, I refuse to answer.
America, I want to tell you about my mother.
I swear to you this never wasn't political.
She fought on the front lines of the second wave
  and never said a word.
She's still there not saying the words she never
  said before.
America, I'm still listening.
I'm a rat-faced son of a bitch and I know how to
  listen.

When will my genius buy my kid's groceries?
Our obese are starved for nutrients.
America, this is not irony.
My sister called just now from France and I told
  her I was writing to you and she
said fine and make sure you tell about what we're
  doing here.
America, this is for my sister who is working to
  the bone. Her feet are broken.
And, America, she's not alone and she's not really
  in France.
America, this is for my sister who is not in France
  and my aunt who's never going
there. This is for my uncle with cancer and the
  Mexican guy pushing the shopping cart telling
  me "Hola." This is for the homeless guy selling
  newspapers in the rain, because I swear to you it
  is still raining here.
And I have always been writing to you. From the
  Northwest forests, leaned up against a tree. From
  the Mighty Mississip marching in an Independence
  Day parade. Whose independence?
Let me tell me you.
I'm putting my white ass to the fucking blade.

            (for all you guys)
I'm with you in Portland, Stephen, walking through
Laurelhurst Park putting the future on a scale
from one to ten, ten being all of it and me wondering how any of it can add up to the dancing moment. I'm with you in Portland, where the streets
are lined with cousins. I'm with you in Portland,
where we eat pizza and run for our lives. I'm with
you in Portland, where basketball is the national
pastime. I'm with you in Portland, when the venom
asks my plans and there's spit on my shoe. My plan
is to run down the middle of the field and answer
only to the last man in my way. Fall back. I'm with
you in Portland, where the soggy ground squishes

through your toes and the sun never rises above the clouds. I'm with you under the firs breathing moss wind and rose water. I'm with you in Portland, in the middle of the street walking home jacket stretched across shoulders. I'm with you in Portland, up early fertile as can be and everywhere still to go. I'm with you on the airplane banking around the north side of Hood. I'm with you at the Skidmore Fountain sitting on cobblestone waiting for the sun to rise. I'm with you, friends, in Forest Park kicking maple leaves. I'm with you at Mississippi Pizza, Chris Marshall, singing the blues. I'm with you in America, Chris Marshall, where every song is ours. I'm with you in the hospital, Ralph. I'm with you on your nighttime rounds, Sister. I'm with you still running through the sawdust park. I'm with you in Grant Park falling down bleeding and getting back up. I'm with you at Produce Row playing my own pint glass jazz radical. I'm with you on Burnside carving my manifesto in wood trying to stop traffic. I'm walking with you to the river where today maybe we jump. I'm with you in Portland, where lumberjacks once grew on trees. I'm with you on Sandy Boulevard, where Grandpa Steve and Grandma Cookie are still piloting an American-made machine. I'm with you in the enclaves and the sanctuaries, the marshes and the woods, the islands and the forgotten pockets. I'm staring in the window, I'm invisible in the dark. I'm with you on the water and under the bridge. I'm floating with you. I'm with you in the sauna where the fat man means well. I'm with you in Portland when the bridge is up and the tunnels lead off into some vanquished night. I'm with you on the couch and in the back of the van. I'm with you driving up the hill, the backseat full of tennis rackets. I'm with you in present tense. I'm with you during goodbye hugs and quivering lips. I'm with you under stars and slowly waving hips. I'm with you in Portland, where fog is a texture, where city streetlights twinkle manically. I'm with you in the ruins and on the fire escape that comes after. Portland, I'm with you when the earth quakes. Portland, peyote sundown fir tree pedestal. Pedestrian right of way, Mt. Tabor eruption. I'm with you, Portland. I am everything your regrets. Portland, I'm with you at the Fox Tower talking to Todd Haynes at dusk. I'm with you at Powell's, where City Lights books are still read with great devotion. I'm with you in Portland, where all roads converge just on the far side of the horizon, always eluding. Zen rotunda Southeast samsara sitting hippie cows. Heroin grind Elliott Smith smile rockstar ghetto. I'm with you in Portland, face down on the sidewalk. I'm with you in the puddles and the small lakes splashing. I'm with you feeding ducks on the lookout for coyotes. I'm with you where the wild things come down from the hills and we lie in Portland waiting. I lie with you on the hard ground bones pressing down earth pressing up. I'm with you in Portland, where old ladies make sandwiches. I'm with you on the full midnight ride across town the Steel Bridge industry banging terrifically as we walk on. I'm with you, Garon, on those uncontained nights that spill out of our mouths and flow to the lowest point, the source never running out of material, the rate increasingly rapidly the closer one gets to the shoes on the ground. All you guys know what's being said, I've been there with you and seen the recognition in the way you leap and sometimes don't stop when we wake up in some mysterious basement I'm the first one up you're not far behind this goes on because it must. We are with you in Portland in our dreams and in yours.

CHAPTER 10: I DON'T BELIEVE IN DISCIPLINE
[Birthday - Winter Break]

The Vulnerable American Male is NOT OK ALL CAPS. I met him in Portland. In Maui. He told me. He's not OK. I gave him a ride home from the bar. Yes, the Vulnerable American Male is at the bar this minute in need of a ride.

Ten cuidado.

My uncle thinks the "I" doesn't exist in time and space, only objects can, only "me." My cousin thinks the work is for whom the work is for. His girlfriend doesn't recognize a big divide between theory and practice.

If we were going to insert a Jan Estep image into the text at this point it would look like this:

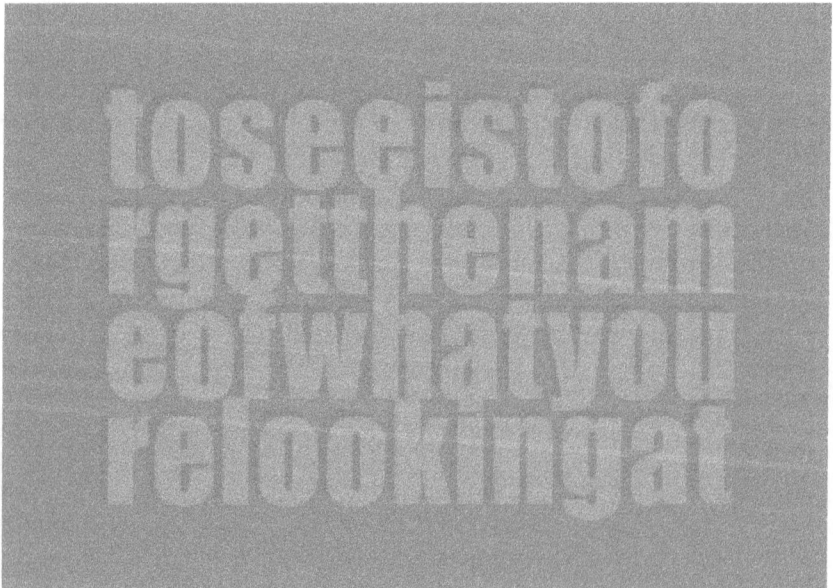

toseeistoforgetthenameofwhatyourelookingat

Estep is a Buddhist, too. Maybe. I'm interviewing her with B.'s help. I'm asking her questions about why she felt the need to write the poem "I Am for an Education." How bad have things gotten that someone had to write this. As if we don't already know. And thank goodness. One of the things we're here to do is cultivate our gratitude.

Have you ever read a text that was not at root a spiritual text?

Pass the milk. We're here to cultivate gratitude.

It is my birthday. I am trying to be grateful. It will be the year of Larry Bird. I am trying to be grateful. Andre Agassi is Petrified. Poor Moon in the headphones. Pirates about. Subliminal clouds. I am surrounded by love and I don't have to try very hard to be grateful right now.

I was maybe going to get a pedicure with my friend O. before she goes down to Miami to wear cute sandals, but last week on Christmas Eve I needed something to do and ripped off one of my toenails. True story. I'll wait for the pedicure till the snow melts in Minnesota.

Back to the birthday. We had dinner, my family and S.'s, at our old go-to Mexican place. I ate so many beans in my bean chimichanga with rice & beans plus chips with bean dip that I had to fight like hell to squeeze the cake and peppermint ice cream in too. I've always been a fighter. Two of my good friends joined us for dessert. They stood on either side of me, arms over shoulders, and danced. It was a dark winter night. Somewhere, people were crashing cars and buying houses, life in some cases going on, in some cases not. They danced and I rested my feet. There really were a great deal of beans in my belly.

Sometimes we must fart to remember who we are. But in this case the beans weren't making me fart. S. and I went with the two dancers to the bar to meet some other friends. I said one beer, but three hours later it wasn't about beer and nothing we were saying could be written off as chatter.

I hugged the Vulnerable American Male for three breaths in the middle of the street while the subliminal clouds watched, and right then he was OK. Never better.

The next day S. and I flew to Minnesota. The Portland we leave is never the Portland we return to. In the weeks before school starts back up I need to get my thesis pretty well together so I can give it to two more readers for feedback, and so I don't have too much to do while I'm in classes. Before getting on the plane I mentioned to my family that I fantasize about dropping out. I haven't told them much about the program, so they were surprised. In Minnesota, I received an email from my dad saying [. . .] He too is someone who is attracted to "education" and repulsed by it. Do you blame him? But before I can turn to the thesis, *that* thesis, I have another migraine. I'm writing for my life here and I have another migraine. I wake up in the morning and it starts coming on within the hour. I take medicine and go back to bed. S. practices Reiki on me between naps. I throw up. I throw up. I have fear. It used to be that when I migrained I could appreciate almost enjoy the heightened sensitivity to sensation. But this is my fourth migraine in four months and what I get now is scared. Scared that it won't end, scared that the next one will come too soon, scared that I'll never get to my work, my work. Scared that if these don't go away ...

Before I can return to the thesis, though, *that* thesis, I have to stall. I have to write a proposal for another book. I have to write an article about politics for a popular magazine that makes me all sorts of gross-feeling. Why do I have to? To learn important facts and figures. A thing is a thing. And a thing that is not a thing is not a thing. And you don't know that till you know it.

But wait, there's more. What am I doing with my life? #duh. I have to give the cat her due attention. I have to walk outside long enough to suck some of the oil out of my skin. I have to give blood. I have to shake these rattley bones. I have to celebrate. But instead I fall asleep and the next day innocently going about my business I run into him again.

I meet the Vulnerable American Male. He's in Minnesota now. And the first thing he does is hug me and invite me into the hearth. His young son is snuggled up with mother by the fire. Primal. Outside it is roughly no degrees. In here, in here . . . the Vulnerable American Male brings me a beer and we discuss our imperfect egos. Our wives sit at our feet and admire us. That last part is a lie. We are all of trying to figure out how to live.

Did I mention that I've stopped shaving? It's winter in Minnesota. What are you thinking? My beard is itchy. My beard, such as it is. S. is not pregnant, in case you were wondering.

The cold is coming. The real winter is coming. It's negative eleven right now and falling fast. I went to a coffee shop. I went to another coffee shop. I went to another coffee shop. At a fourth coffee shop I drank a mocha. It tasted like metal. Fuck it, time to start the thesis. I take out a book and read Barry Lopez. "It is painful and old news that human life is in trouble." "The ability to feel awe before what is unfathomable and beyond human control . . ." "Writing, too, is a social as well as an artistic act." Damn, that's what I was trying to say.

K. emails about a "final notice" to have input on who the university hires to be the new nonfiction faculty. It is also the first notice. I say yes. This place, this place. Maybe there's hope. Dangerous hope.

My sister had a severe allergic reaction to a

nut in her cake last night. Was she scared for her life? Was she scared for her life?

CHAPTER 11: OFF TECHNOLOGY
[Today → Yesterday: An Interruption]

At this point in the manuscript I'm switching to
the typewriter* I just bought with money I received
from my parents for Christmas. It's a Correctronic
GX-6750 Electronic Typewriter made by the brand
brother, which is intentionally uncapitalized. I
am making this switch for several vague yet related reasons all having to do with a chronic,
if low-grade, unease about the role of so-called
"technology" (really I just mean electronics) in
my life. Though the writing in in vivo is pretty
free form, I'm interested in the ways in which the
typewriter will free me up to compose. The ways it
restricts me are obvious. I cannot cut and paste.
I must proceed more or less sequentially or develop an elaborate system of notation to account for
deviance. Again, this is not so much a problem for
the current project, which was formatted on screen
to appear as if typewritten (use of Courier New,
primarily) and controlled by the time constraints
in a manner parallel with the constraints imposed
by material existence: the paper turns through
the typewriter in one direction only, there is no
practical backing up. What does down on the page
stays on the page. A sense of permanence. A sense
that what we do here matters. And that it matters.
Our existence leaves traces. Though in vivo has
been from the beginning a low-tech use of high-tech
tools, the ways in which the tools of technology
shape the artifacts produced with them is serious.

---

* Before, that is, going back and typing it up as an electronic version.

I have noticed in myself in other projects an in-
creasing tendency toward collage and fragmenting,
toward short sentences and fast-arriving conclusions. I have noticed in myself an inability to
sustain a long line of thought. For someone who
has essentially staked his life on his ability to
concentrate, this is a matter of some concern. A
good craftsman, they say, never blames his tools.
As a way of training myself to use my tools, I'm
attempting to separate myself from them, to feel
what it's like to be by myself, to face the duty
of thinking and writing without having a constant
and pervasive escape pulling at my attention, offering little reward, rewards that are rarely, if
ever, worth their promise. Of course, I'm thinking of the internet here. If I were writing this
on a computer and not on this typewriter I would
have checked my email approximately one million
times since starting this paragraph.* Every pause
to think of the next word affords the occasion
to look for signs that a new email has landed in
my inbox (inbox here referring to all of my in-
boxes, of which you can be sure there are many).
Even as a string of words arises in my mind and
is quickly transmitted to my fingers, my eyes will
dance across the surface of the screen in desperate search of . . . something new. When these new
emails come, as they inevitably do, my mind latch-
es promptly upon what they may bring: news from a
friend (doubtful); news of my breakthrough as a
writer, fame and fortune (I'm always on the brink
of receiving one of these); usually it's boring
and work-related; sometimes it's still an ad or a
listserv thing, though I've tried to get off of
them all--in any case, whatever I was trying to do
in language is long gone from my attention and as I
find my way back to it I presumably find myself into
new, if halting, possibilities that the pre-dis-

---

* This claim confirmed 6/3/14.

traction momentum would have prevented. Is this a
good thing? Sometimes probably. You can't rebut
with a counterfactual, but I'll tell you what it
feels like. It feels like my thoughts are as scat-
tered as my eyes and I'm so busy moving between
things that I never notice what the things themselves are. I trust you know the condition. Maybe
the reason everybody has ADHD now is that everyone
has ADHD now. We've effectively built it into our
culture and called it, what, efficiency, multitask-
ing, freedom . . . Call me old-fashioned. The more
time I spend on the internet the harder it is for
me to remember how to live away from it. That's
not the old-fashioned part. The old-fashioned part
is that this strikes me as a potential problem.
If what it means to be human is constantly changing along with technology, so be it, but some of
us have to wonder then which technologies we want
to choose. Which futures. Not everyone I know is
a writer. I know TV addicts and drug addicts and
shopping addicts, too. (None of these categories
is exclusive.) So what's wrong with the internet?
Here's one thing the internet tells me: when my
new typewriter is sitting on my desk alongside
my laptop and I think it's time to do some writing, the typewriter says, "You can use me for your
writing," and the laptop says, "You can use me
for your writing and you can do all these other
things (including italics)." Those other things
are essentially the internet calling out to what's
weak in me. Clearly a tool with more functions
is a better tool. That's the American way. It's
the Swiss Army Knife. I cut my thumb once, badly,
with a Swiss Army Knife. It bled as if it were cut
by a regular knife. What's the difference, I can
hear the past asking me. The difference is I never
would have cut myself with a standard knife. To do
one thing well is enough. I feel as if I am in a
battle for my attention. I think it's mine and I'm
willing to fight to protect it. Lately I have taken

to imposing internet breaks on myself. I leave my computer and my phone at home and go out into the world on my own. This is what passes for living dangerously today. Laugh or pity, it is a bravery that takes cultivation. I'm not giving up. Often, when I go out I take a book so I can see what it's like to read only the words on the page. No links, no looking stuff up, no thinking of something else to read that's more interesting or easier, no forgetting what I started out doing, no email. Just the words on the page and what I think about them. I'm teaching myself how to read, how to pay attention, how to live, and how to accept my own private limitations. It's these limitations, after all, that define me. I would rather fail to fully know myself than spend the entirety of my life trying to escape myself. It's scary in here, but it's much scarier to think that death is the only thing you have to look forward to. You can chase your tail till you drop. Plenty of people do. But you don't have to. When I go on these internet breaks to read, the books I've been taking with me of late have been *Walden* and the collected works of Aldo Leopold. And the longer I sit with these men the stronger I grow and the easier it is to sit. I haven't taken out my phone in an hour, two hours, three, and I'm still alive. I'm alive. I'm alive.

CHAPTER 12: THE WORK WE DO
[Time Indeterminate: A Continuation]

Speaking of my sister, she's in Rome. She was
blindfolded the other night and taken to the Coliseum. When her eyes were uncovered, the ruins--
they're more than ruins--were revealed to her. It
is understood, yes, this was her first visit to the
Coliseum, her first visit to Rome, her first wandering visit to Europe. She sent a photograph of herself with two fellow travelers leaned up against
that statue of Zeus flinging coins (them) over
their shoulders into the water, making the promises that are satisfied in the act, promises that
this moment will linger as long as it deserves
to, promises that our intentions are pure, promises that we won't, even as we eventually return
home, become trapped there, won't forget what it
is to have our eyes of experience opened so that
we may learn what everyone else is talking about-
-a starting point to determining whether whatever
it is they are talking about is something we want
to take with us. We will take only what we need
and our needs are unique. I wrote her an email in
which I said, "Don't go to the Louvre, and if you
do don't see the *Mona Lisa*, and if you do don't
tell me about it. Tell me what's happening in your
heart, in the leisurely afternoons, in your understanding of what it means to build a life." Two
things occurred to me after sending this email.
One, it is easier for me to hurt my sister than
it is for me to hurt anyone else. I can even do
it when I'm trying to do the opposite. Two, I am
as prone to cliché as anyone, sophisticated as I

think mine are.

Why mention this here? She is in Europe to do work. A kind of work that is too often neglected, the work of cultivating the self. She left a stable career in Portland to travel here to Minnesota, now to Europe, next to Mexico, before returning home to see about starting a new career. Why mention it here? Because I admire it and because it is a reminder of what I'm attempting to explore in this work. Namely, that life is a project of constant revision. The parallels between writing and living come naturally for this reason. A work of art should be a work of life, and vice versa. If this experiment is going to pay off* it must locate similar turning points in the life of "I." The courage to walk away from something safe in search of something better. To feel the urge to create art is to demonstrate dissatisfaction with the current state of affairs. And if the analogy holds, it's also to demonstrate dissatisfaction with the state of the self. (That feels like an overreach. I should edit that out or amend it such that it refers to memoir only. Better? A little. Still doesn't feel quite right. Can't be boxed in by analogy.†) Stepping out. To have a human mind is to be capable of level jumping. Hey, we're over here. Pity the kid who doesn't move fast enough. Joke's on you. But we must leave trails if we're ever to be followed. We want sometimes to be followed, but by who or by whom? By who or by whom?

---

* But it pays off too if it "proves" the null case, right?
† I feel a digression coming on. We think in patterns. We live in patterns. Our syntax dictates the content of our thoughts. If there is X and Y then very often there must also by Z, not because things come in threes but because the rhythm of three is usually better than the rhythm of two. Just as the programmer thinks in "if, then, else," I, for example, write in "this, but, so" constructions. I can help it, but I usually don't, so I end up with a distinctive syntax that limits the kinds of things I can say. Analogy, syntax, rhythm, rhyme, logic, on and on it goes, where it stops. Silence.

Before Italy, my sister was in Lyon, staying with our cousin, her partner, and their baby
daughter. That cousin's father has cancer and not
a lot of time. In the summer of 2012 when I started working on the book about Oregon, and again in
the summer of 2013, I talked with this uncle and
my dad's sister to whom he is married about ideas
of where to travel and what to investigate. One of
the pieces from the book is roadtrip prose poem
thing that was partly based on a list of favorite
places in Oregon that she gave me and stories of
adventure that he told me. I wanted to have a nice
way to share it with them, so I produced a chapbook
version. As of today, it is on its way from the
printer. I might not have done this when I did if
it were not for the pressure of time. This aunt and
uncle's son is the cousin who said, "the writing
is for who the writing is for."

This is a continuation of the same chapter, but I wanted a fresh page to transition from thinking about my uncle's process of dying and my trying to make a gift for him to writing that is not a gift (at least not in the same way).

I read an article in an online magazine that addressed a subject that is of personal interest to me. The article, I thought, had some problems. I wrote to the editor and said I could write on the same topic and come up with something better. This was part of my project to come up with more paid assignments so I could figure out whether it might ever be viable for me to support myself as a freelancer. The editor told me to go for it, so I wrote something. I realized quickly that while it was something I could do, it wasn't something I particularly enjoyed doing. It wasn't *for* the reader; it was for me, so I could get paid. I went ahead with it because I said I would and because doing something for money doesn't make it bad, it just makes it a job. But at the same time I knew I wasn't doing my soul any favors.

At the same time I pitched other stories and discovered that if I keep pitching I can keep finding outlets and in some cases paychecks. It might be possible for this to turn into (not a career, I don't know anyone who believes in careers anymore, but:) a way to support myself. It would be an awful lot of hustle, but it would be possible. All of this in the context of the end of school being in sight. Everyone is getting a bit squirmy about what's next. Whether you like grad school or not, at least it's grad school and comes with a small paycheck. Some people are applying for fellowships and residencies; others are applying for more grad school. Some want to teach. Pretty much everyone wants to keep writing. I want to keep being involved in the making of books, or the living breathing literary culture otherwise. I applied for a job as events planner for a local bookstore.

Nope. I applied for an entry-level position at the newspaper. Nope. I think of teaching, but the workload of a bad job and the politics of a good one deflate me about equally.

ENTRE

Let me tell you about a visit from someone I admire. She comes for the day and I volunteer to be one of her escorts. There is a break between events in her schedule. I invite her to coffee. She, the other escort, and I go to a local coffee hangout. She is one of my favorite living writers. Today I'm not interested in that. Today I'm interested in how she carries herself. Poise. Confidence. Grace. These words come to mind. We talk in a somewhat casual, somewhat formal way about writing, teaching, grad school, etc. She mentions Joan Didion. I mention that I've recently reread "In Bed" because I'm working on an essay about migraines. Then I make a strange joke about how reading Didion on migraines makes me question why I'm trying to do it too. It's the kind of thing people sometimes say to appear humble or to make others feel comfortable. It's the kind of bullshitty thing I take pride in not saying, but I must have been nervous. She, to her credit, called my bullshit for what it was. It would have been easy to let it slide or to speak encouragingly (condescendingly), but she did neither. I don't have a chance to talk with her much after coffee, but I continue to watch how she carries herself. The thing I notice above others is the seamlessness in how she speaks about writing, teaching, living--these are all connected for her, sincerely so. Her writing has always struck me as uncommonly wise. Her presence is similarly wise but there's more. She's uncommonly authentic as well. Her performance of self admits of no cracks. Genuine, stable, even mountain-like, I could go on a run of adjectives here. I won't. Instead, I'll

turn to imagining the room from her POV. Being the
calm presence in the swirling silliness of extreme
ego play. Can you sit down with someone and offer
them what you have to give? Do you know what it is
that you have to give/ And what do you not have?
Patience, patience, patience.

The same day, I get a set of interview questions
about my chapbook in here. One of the questions
has to do with what I learned from that project and
where it's leading me. I won't mention this in the
interview, but one place it's led is here. in vivo
is in many ways a continuation of the concerns of
in here. The self, memoir, time, the sprawliness
of these things. It answers in a way, too, some of
the concerns of this chapter. This is not a piece
for a popular magazine. I don't expect anyone will
pay me for it. Its rewards must be its their own.
And they are. What will I do after grad school as
I look for ways to remain a writer? I hope (among
whatever else) stuff like this, stuff that I know
who or whom it is for. Me, yes, but also you. You
are here with me this time, reader. For the time
being, this is what I have to offer you.

CHAPTER 13: PROBLEM WITH AUTHORITY
[February 6, 2014 & February 8, 2014]

February 6. 2:30 p.m. ██████████████████
███
███
███
███
██
███
███
███
██
███
███
███
███████████████████████████████████████
███
███
██████████████████████████████████████
██
███
███
███
███████████████████████████████████████
███
██████████████████
██████████████████████ [Note to self: When I revise, I
need to show the good judgment to delete/redact
most of this section. It won't do to be bitter, it
won't do to be bitter.]
    What this has to do with the project at hand
is that I was already angered afterward when ███
███
███
██████████████████████████ (This is approximately the experience of everyone ██████████████████████████████

██

██

██

██

██

██

██

██

██

██

██

██

███████████████████████████████* and
asked B. and F. to meet me to discuss my thesis.

Feb. 8, 3:08 p.m. Common Roots. B. & F.: tea & beer.

The reasons to switch to make <u>in vivo</u> my thesis include thinking it would be easier / better / more
interesting to present and feeling like the Oregon thing doesn't really fit in the context of the
program anymore. The first one is true, but that
in itself isn't a good enough reason. The second
is overthought--a thesis is just whatever someone
is working on. Reasons not to switch are that an
environmentally inclined professor has generously
offered to read the whole manuscript in his spare
time (he's reading it now) and he's doing so in the

*████████████████████

████████████████████████

████████████████████████████

██████████

███████████████████████████

████████████████

██████████████████████████████████

██████████████████████████████████

███████████████

██████████████████████

████████████████████

███████████████████

context of it being a thesis. Does that matter? I
don't know. I'd have to ask him.

When I tell B. and F. at Common Roots that I'm
frustrated and want to switch projects they understand. Their advice, though, ultimately is that I
should stick with Oregon. Those essays are good
and could benefit from further attention and maybe
turn into a good book. *This project*, which I've
now described to them, sounds cool and is worth
pursuing, but the nature of it puts the timeline
in question. To finish it by April would be arbitrary and a little stymieing. Better to stick with
Oregon and do in vivo on the side. They are right,
as I knew, but what was most convincing was when
B. said to remember I can talk about whatever I
feel like in the presentation. It doesn't have to
be about anything but what I feel like having it
be about.

There are facts and there is how we think about
them. The Stoic doesn't wish for anything to be
other than it is. The wise man does what needs to
be done and doesn't waste precious energy on ex-
cessive thinking. Silence might be the most profound response to grief; it might also be the most
profound response to fear, to doubt, to self.

Consider these ambiguous notes I find on a scrap
of paper I couldn't have written more than a few
weeks ago but don't recall having written or what
they might have meant:

how to think:
a thing that happens to be being done
a job that doesn't pay well but that does pay an
  opportunity unrealized
what we do with our time becomes our lives syntax
  dreams
the humans are sick and the empire's collapsing

CHAPTER 14: OVERHEATED
[5 a.m.]

Last night I watched *Synecdoche, New York*.
   A movie without sequel, it put me in a sick dark
place. I slept, briefly, because I was tired, but
the sic ness pursued me. Art. To capture to drama-
tize to document the collapse of a human being. An
ouroboros of death. Decay. The slow rot of self-
digestion.
   There's nothing to say about the film. It only
allows feelings that are already buried to unbury.
I'm thinking about patterns, patterns of thinking.
Whole new frameworks for how one arranges experience.

[The thesis presentation has become the event into
which I've distilled all of my mixed feelings
about this program--and my uncertainties about how
to present myself as an artist. I'm writing this
section inside brackets because it helps me to
imagine that I'm not "really" writing it, that it
doesn't "really" mean as much to me as it feels
like it does, that it would be the easiest thing
in the world to delete this paragraph from the archives of my history, that this is a liminal and
incompletely formalized space that exists somewhere sideways of reality. It is as if the presentation is an asymptote of experience. Everything
there gets magnified to an impossible limit. Mani-
fested in my individual and finite human presence,
that means what? A breakdown in consciousness, a
panic attack, wherein the subject "I" is literally (close to literally) obliterated by the mo-

ment. That sounds crazy. It could mean no big deal whatsoever. Play it cool. It could mean wowing the audience--anything is possible. But I'm thinking about patterns. What would it mean for the presentation to be some thing (not for the audience, for me) that I have not yet conceived, something that for me would appear from a place outside my normal circle of experience . . . what if I were someone else? The more I think about it, the more I think the presentation is the event around which this project hinges and will be its culminating chapter. It feels like the presentation has always been shaping the project and was the cause of the temptation to switch to this project. The questions I still face going forward include: Why does it matter so much to me? What to do about it? Being in front of a crowd concentrates the ambivalence I feel. Ambivalence can be an important place from which to make art. It allows one to honestly explore his subject. However, unless one can find the appropriate way in which to get meta on it, it's not a very useful place from which to present that art, honest though it may be. One of my difficulties in getting on in the world: honest though I may be. What I'm inclined to do here is push through, grind it out, bear it. This is how I've lived my life, somehow trusting a utopia of self is one day coming--patterns of thought that run deeper even than my "I," my culture. But there is the brain and maybe my suffering is one beta-blocker away from being vanquished. And there is the mind and maybe my suffering is something that can be transformed into . . . into what? . . .]

Because of the time, I'm typing this section on the computer instead of the typewriter. The typewriter is too aggressive for this early in the morning. It would assault my brain, make violence to the air, not to mention wake S. One thing this laptop has going for it is the quietness of its keys. And one thing that is worth mentioning here is how this quiet typing is proving effective in quieting my mind. It's nearly 6 a.m. now and I am not so overheated. I mean this literally. I've put on sweats, sandals, and even a hat. The temperature outside is -2 and will up to 0 by the time I go to meditation at Dharma Field in a few hours. But less literally, working on this project [even if in brackets] sooths me and I wonder if what it narrates is not so much my insanity as the way I modify that insanity/suffering toward productive ends. This project can--I don't know, why not?--give meaning to the suffering the program/the presentation produce in me. I can outcontextualize them. Which raises again for me the question of function. S. asked me at one point how this is different from a blog or a journal, and while pride makes me say it's neither, the fact that I used a word like "sooth" makes me wonder if this isn't all for my purposes, which I think 1) is/will be answered in the framing / packaging / presentation, not in the "content" itself, as a thing in art can be two things at least or more; and 2) debilitating to consider and entirely at odds with purported "soothingness." Self-defeatingly so. That painful digression aside, I feel better. Not to be fully discounted.

LATER

After writing the above (and we're back on typewriter now), I went to Dharma Field to meditate and hear Steve Hagen give a dharma talk. As I listened to the talk what B. said about talking about whatever I wanted to talk about was hovering in the back of my consciousness and mixing with Hagen's words in a relaxed state. This was not a Zen of single-minded focus; this was a Zen of openness to the stuff of consciousness, which mixed freely until suddenly I recognized how I could combine

B.'s advice with my interests--the kind of thing Hagen was talking about, only applied to nonfiction writing: what is that mysterious "I" that we take for granted as nonfiction writers? After my heart-felt bows, I got coffee and a cupcake and wrote out an outline of the entire presentation. Maybe I will change it. Maybe I will not. For now, there's that.

CHAPTER 15: MORE PROBLEMS WITH AUTHORITY
[February 13, 2014 - March 31, 2014]

THE CONTENTS OF THIS CHAPTER HAVE BEEN WITHHELD.

CHAPTER 16: ON THE MARGINS
[April Fool's Day - Earth Day]

EFACE

I STARTED THIS work   having publication in
mind.
             however, I did not conceal from myself
doubts which seemed to stand in the way of publication: mainly consideration for certain persons
          living
              my body and   personal
fate   value both
science and   religious truths. I
   e face   such   ration al personal issues

WITHOUT □ , WHAT IS THE SELF?

I have decided to apply the methods of my <u>in vivo</u>
project to my Marginalia seminar paper and include
my marginalia seminar paper in my <u>in vivo</u> project.*

---

* For those reading the present essay as a seminar paper, a
few prefatory remarks are in order. <u>in vivo</u> is a memoir that
begins, "Everyone knows memoir is about the past. ¶ But what
if it's not?" From that the rest nearly follows. All that's
left is to discover what that following includes. The work
seeks its subject in (allowing for sleep, breaks, breakdowns,
hiatuses, vacations, trysts, etc.) real time. Whatever events
occur in the life of the author are fashioned into the unfolding story. What makes it a memoir, then, and not a diary? Only
the kinds of eyes through which its author, The Synthesis,
sees--eyes straining against the slant glare at the window
to make out objects beyond the field of vision--straining and
straining and . . . . .

There will not be, as there never is, one without the other. (To assume a bounded one is to have already assumed an infinite number of finitudes.)

This essay happily joins in such assumptions, as it is written, and all writing joins—it joins a conversation that jumps media and retreats into the ether only at the point when there's no one yet to record, repeat, retrace. As soon, though, as there is this one, there are the rest of us, here writing, here talking: hear writing, hear talking. So when there is one . . . and before there is one, there is not yet *before*, only:

The other aspect of this essay, which is the nothing that is not yet a nothing, which prefers silence and resists being written. It will be this part of the essay that cannot be written that is nevertheless the most important part of it: the part written around not in avoidance but in an attempt at circumscription. What eludes the text? Escapes without moving? Disappears in stillness? Was never written and never even written upon?

Just over a month ago, for a short assignment in Marginalia class that asked us to examine a passage from the class reading, I turned in to Professor Leslie Morris these

Notes on Lil Wayne's "God Bless Amerika" and Other Martian Songs of a Minor Literature

Furthermore, not a human being, neither from this planet nor of it, bearing no relation, even, to Father Time or Mother Nature.* The truth he speaks, a foreign language to us (whoever we are). And the origin, then, alien, and remaining so despite transliteration. Google the lyrics, sing along to the hook, improvise your own version; the song never starts, never stops, only plays and plays

---

* LM: "Unclear?"

through the perpetual present moment of the materially nearly independent interent.

Right now, and right now, the alien is speaking. As in Dylan, as in Derrida, there is "no outside the text" for Wayne. The seemingly infinite and hyper-generative and self-generating catalogue,[*] the performance of "artist" (of "art"),[†] the purple drank,[‡] the ink spilled over skin[§]--the body, the music, the self: all equally and undifferentiatably text. Wayne literally embodies textuality as he literalizes Derrida's claim that "the materiality of being is textual." The figure of Wayne, which his audience knows (only) textually, forces them/us to confront the question of what a text even is, where it starts and where it ends--or how we read a text that does neither.

A text such as Wayne's pursues the infinite and fills, eventually spills out of, the "cramped space" of a minor literature. If the literature of Black English is always necessarily political and collective, then the literature of a sublanguage (of

---

[*] Debuting age twelve as a member of B.G.; B.G. transitioning into Hot Boys and during teenage years; solo debut at seventeen; eleven solo albums over the next fifteen years; two EPs; nineteen mixtapes; one remix album; collabos; more guest spots than anyone since 2Pac's ghost. None of this even hinting at what's in the vaults. Wayne famously lives in the studio, his life one ongoing recording session, breaks between songs introduced basically when he stops to refill his purple cup or roll another blunt.

[†] In interviews, in documentaries, in music videos, as in Dylan, as in Derrida, Wayne performs being; style becomes substance; the artist becomes a way of speaking becomes a way of being.

[‡] Ubiquitous styrofoam cup of a piece with the "material." Wayne as product, inspiration in a cup or from god; seizures caused by the drug and/or the epilepsy; art caused by . . . . .

[§] Too many hundreds of tattoos to count, covering his body and reaching over his lips into his gums; the piercings; the grill=the "human" body subverted to the cause of . . . the (not-blank) slate on which is written . . . the material transcended for the sake of . . . . .

the South, of New Orleans in particular) is more
so, and a language so sub- as to permit of a single
speaker, all the more. The space Wayne lives in is
so cramped, he is as if the entire world, which
allows him the opportunity denied most authors of
minor literatures: to be fully individuated from
his language partners (he effectively has none,
only foreign audience) and therefore uncramped by
its limitations. Is this still a minor literature,
or now a major alien tongue?

Deleuze and Guattari ask "How to become a no-
mad and an immigrant and a gypsy in relation to
one's own language?" Wayne explodes the question
by leaving the planet. He's an alien to his audience, to this planet, to his own words. He's
free from them. No one expects Wayne to "speak
for black people" anymore (as so many people are
expected to, or are assumed to be doing at all
times); no one even asks him to speak for rap anymore, or for the South, or for New Orleans. If, as
Deleuze and Guattari write, it is "the glory of
this sort of minor literature--to be the revolu-
tionary force for all literature," Wayne becomes
that force through sheer weirdness and unworldly
prolificity.* The example of Wayne's liberation is

---

* For most artists, mixtapes now are the filler between major
releases to maintain a presence in the short memories of an
online audience; they are marginal works that occur on the
blank spaces outside the main text of albums. When Wayne came
up the mixtape functioned more as a way of building buzz to
allow for an eventual album. Wayne was the artist to make
himself (as a solo artist after his early group work) through
mixtapes but then continue to produce mixtapes alongside his
studio albums. For him there's no meaningful difference between mixtapes and studio albums. He continually composes his
text on whatever surfaces happen to be available, not caring
for much outside the work occurring now. This claim is supported by the fact that much of his best work appears on mixtapes. The marginal work for him is as important as the work
it's marginal to. Because there's so much of Wayne (as with
Dylan), he's at once impossible to pin down to any particular
instance of his work. At the same time, his work works syn-

to escape the minority status of one's work by building something bigger than empire.*

to which she responded: "This is an interesting start to a paper--especially your reading of Deleuze/Guattari--but I'm left unclear about where you are going with it."

    A reasonable concern. I wasn't sure where I was going with it, either, wasn't particularly planning on going anywhere--getting "somewhere" being less of a concern for me than keeping moving; I'm just trying to think out loud here and draw connections between things that interest me, trusting, as I trust, that all roads will lead somewhere and we'll find out where when we get there. The product/artifact always simultaneously both complete and in progress, depending on the direction one is facing. E.g., all notes (it could be said) lead to Wayne, and all Waynes lead to . . .
  ..

A week or two later in class, Professor Morris asked us to email her with proposals for our final

---

echodically for the itself. There is no context to Wayne. If he were a book, you could read him upside-down, backwards, starting from any page you like. Like a foreign language, he demands emersion and resists mastery (except through participation).
* LM: "Can you say more about how you want to link Dylan & Derrida?"

    S: Sure. In Dylan's case, what I have in mind is the multitude of Dylans there are no. Since no singular Dylan is definitive (and yet so many are distinctive), what becomes essential in him is anti- essentialism. It's the variety of Dylan that constitutes the concept of Dylan. With Derrida, I'm thinking of that phenomenon wherein those discussing Derrida invariably come to imitate the style of Derrida, the playfulness, the attention to sound and pattern, the reflexive and discursive movement of the sentences, and so on. It is as if Derrida (and discussions of his work) reveal the inseparability of form and content. In either case, the style is the substance.

papers. I wrote:

Dear Professor Morris,

In class you said you want our final papers to be related to our work. I hope that means you'll consider something like the following appropriate.

Last year I published a chapbook of "anti-memoirs" under a pseudonym. Since then, I've been taking notes for what I hope will be that pseudonym's follow-up book/chapbook. The idea I've had (and apologies for the vagueness of this) for awhile is that my final paper for class would be a chapter in/from/for this work. This makes a certain amount of sense since one of the things this new work is interested in is playing with form. It's trying to be a memoir written forward- rather than backward-looking, and the form is influenced by the content of its section's moment. Meaning, I suspect, an essay/ chapter written relating to marginalia would employ margins as locations for writing.

The challenge I feel like I'm facing is what the jumping off point is. Maybe one of the texts from class (*Book of Margins, Book of Disquiet*). Or maybe I'd work out from my short paper, doing something like annotating an excerpt from Wayne's "body" of work.

There's a Nietzsche quote that I haven't been able to locate yet about how the greatness of the Greeks came from their superficiality.[†] One

---

† "Oh, those Greeks! They knew how to live. What is required for that is to stop courageously at the surface, the fold, the skin, to adore appearance, to believe in forms, tones, words, in the whole Olympus of appearance. Those Greeks were superficial--*out of profundity*. And is not this precisely

idea I have is thinking about that in relation to my claim from the short paper that some people (e.g., Weezy & Derrida) have such style that style in many ways overwhelms and becomes the content.

What do you think about taking this creative approach to the assignment?

S.

Her response:

Dear S.,

Thanks for your email. Let me clarify a bit what I meant when I said I hoped your final papers would be somehow germane to all of your work outside the class. I meant simply not that I want you to write about something or texts that we are not reading, but that I hoped each of you would find a way to make the class productive for your own thinking about your research projects. I hope this clarifies. To that end, it seems to me that two texts we will be reading in the next few weeks are of possible interest to you: The Canvas (as it deals with a fictitious/forged memoir) and also Pessoa's Book of Disquiet, an extended rumination on the "heteronyms" created by Pessoa (which are not the same as Pessoa himself). Does this make sense?

lm

---

what we are again combing back to, we daredevils of the spirit who have climbed the highest and most dangerous peak of present thought and looked around from up there--we who have looked *down* from there? Are we not, precisely in this respect, Greeks? Adorers of forms, of tones, of words? And therefore--*artists*?"

Yes. And no. I wrote to a classmate for help interpreting.

"Do you read it that I can or cannot do the creative thing?"

"I couldn't tell either. She was open, but also 'no' about it. I honestly think you should do your chapter, it's a matter of framing it in a way she approves of."

I wonder if she will approve of this.[*]

Lacking a "research project,"[†‡] I will endeavour to think about and draw connections between some of the class's texts in a manner that satisfies the requirements of the academic expectations while remaining productive for what I do have: a [this] project.

Specifically, then, what I want to look at is how the self is presented, represented, critiqued, problematized, fragmented, erased, exchanged, quieted, et cetera, et cetera, and so on, in three of the books we read in the Marginalia seminar--Benjamin Stein's *The Canvas*; Daniel Paul Schreber's *Memoirs of My Nervous Illness*; and Fernando Pessoa's *The Book of Disquiet*--paying particular attention to the ways in which 1) the self is necessarily a kind of fiction; and 2) the forms the self takes in memoir are created as they're revealed.

The Canvas ends in the middle. The reader begins from either of the book's sides and progresses toward narrative completion mid-book, whereupon the

---

[*] Classmate: Good luck!

   S. Thanks! I'll let you know.

[†] Or since research for me is a method of creation/participation more than aimed at achieving (un)certain results . . .

[‡] A note on "research": The Marginalia class is taught in the German department and is in the majority composed of super-smart grad students from fields such as German, English, and Art, who are marvels of academic achievement and fluent in the language of scholarship. Additionally, there are four grad-student poets, plus whatever kind of character I am.

book is flipped and read from the other end.* Now a second narrative leads to the same place: *The Canvas* ends where the two narratives meet (in both senses: the narratives themselves lead to each other).†

This reader happened to read first the narrative of Amnon Zichroni, a boy who is, intentionally or not, led astray by his parents from the religious fundamentalism of his community. When he is caught reading Oscar Wilde's *The Picture of Dorian Gray*, he is booted from school and sent to live with his "uncle" in Switzerland, where though still raised under strict Judaism continues to move incrementally closer to secular life. The process of secularization continues in the U.S. and culminates in Zichroni's career, back in Geneva, as a psychoanalyst.

Zichroni makes a good memoirist.‡ He is a smart,

---

* "Toward narrative completion" takes on another meaning as the two narratives (though on collision course) do not finally resolve--the book's narrative (its two narratives) remains headed toward a completion it (they) never reaches (reach). The text resists final conclusion.

† A memoir is always narrated from its midpoint--as the self is always suspended between past and future--and therefore always ends at the midpoint . . . can never be completed . . . Aristotle said we cannot judge a person's happiness until fifty years after death. You may try to describe your own level of happiness, but everything up till now is backstory.

‡ And let's acknowledge that a fictional memoirist saves much hand- wringing: by freeing readers of expectations of correlation with the so-called "real," we get past the distractions and right to the question of how a conscious self understands itself in the funhouse of mirrors of its consciousness, wherever that consciousness lives. ¶ Think what James Frey's *A Million Little Pieces* would be if it were read like this (as he meant for it to be, before his publisher agreed to publish it only under the condition he presented his novel as memoir). Readers could be invited to reflect on whether a self-styled tough-guy's self-understanding had anything worthwhile to offer a reader reckoning with his or her own failures rather than if a month in jail was really a night in the drunk tank. We are spared such fact checking in Zincroni's case because, though he thinks he's real, we do

curious, and eager to make sense of his past. But it is his unusual relationship to memory that really suits him to the form. Physical contact allows Zichroni to sometimes access the memories of the person he is in contact with. First as a boy in Israel, his father. Later, a school friend. With time he develops some control of the skill, but even then when he is powerless to keep the (stolen? borrowed? peeped?) memories from feeling as if his own. For a narrator who says (on the first page, no less) that "it is our memories that make us what we are," the implications for his power are haunting. By tapping into someone's memories, Zichroni does not see them truly or identify with them--he actually *becomes* them.

And yet memory, he reminds us, is unreliable. "Each time we remember, we reshape, filter, separate and connect, add in, take out, and replace the original bit by bit over time through the memory of a memory." So who, then, does he become but a fiction? And who is he in the first place, who is anyone in the book, but, also, a fiction?[*] "Who, then," he asks, "can say what really happened?"

No one can. Raising the question: did anything "really" happen? Appropriately, this becomes the driving plotline of either part of the book. Sticking with Zichroni's story for now, he encounters a violin repairman, Minsky, who shares with Zichroni his story of surviving the Holocaust. Zichroni confirms the trauma through touch, but all he is really able to confirm are the memories of the events, not the events themselves. When Minsky's memoir is disproved by evidence, it does not affect the memory. (Is it possible that someone like James Frey, who offers plenty to oppose (exploitation of other writers, frequent bad writing on his

---

not. Only, it's not quite so simple. See next note.

[*] Reader, do not neglect the analogy. Your narrator, too, is a fiction. Reader, your memories, too, are faulty. Reader, you too are made of lies.

own part) anyway, could have come to believe his lies? And would this make a difference in how we respond to him? A little?) Unlike in *Dorian Gray*, here when the representation is punctured, the "real thing," such as it is, goes on.*

Part of creating a self is determining when and what to share with other selves. As Zichroni narrates, "People decide, speak, and reveal only as much as they themselves want to. But I hadn't even asked for permission. None of them had meant to share their secrets with me." In a way (even if we assume, tenuously, that his accessing memories does not distort them), he steals from his contacts, relieving them of the creative act of choosing what to reveal, a choosing he is otherwise committed to enabling.

"In analysis," he says, "you could put the reins back in their hands--or rather, the pallet and the paintbrush, so they could set a new tone on the canvas of their memories. You could even become a canvas yourself, a projection screen where the patients could sketch possible alternative drafts." The blank canvas, the locus of creation, where little experiments can be run, where the self can

---

* Quick interjection from real life: Minsy's character is not-so-loosely based on Benjamin Wilkomirski, author of the discredited Holocaust memoir *Fragments: Memories of a Wartime Childhood*. Stein met Wilkomirski at a bookstore reading (just as Weschler met Minsky). Stein has said publically that he does not know whether Wilkomirski was lying or may have thought his story was true. How would he know? How would we? Though an extreme case, Fragments forefronts the assumptions of the memoir form. ¶ (And does it not follow, at least as a possibility, that *The Canvas* is not so much a novel that combines two fictional memoirs as it's Benjamin Stein's memoir disguised as a novel that combines two fictional memoirs? He says that Stein is a nom de plume adopted to distance himself from the poetry he published under his given name (which he refuses to reveal) as a young man in East Germany. "They other name is forgotten," he says. "Even I forgot it." It sounds to The Synthesis like the adopted name is a fresh start, a chance to write a new and original past.)

become what it needs to become, even if this means appropriating someone else's memories and painting them onto your canvas--and *Canvas*, where the canvas itself might appropriate your appropriated memories and paint them into it(s)self.

Half of it anyway. Flipping the book over, I found the story Jan Wechsler, who I knew as the journalist who exposed Minsky's memoir. Wechsler, it turns out, has his own problems with identity. Rather than adopting others', though, he has rejected/repressed/forgotten his own. When he discovers that a Jan Wechsler discredited Minsky, it's a slow realization and acceptance that it was he. Wechsler believes that as a writer "No one knows better than I that the boundary between reality and fiction in every story runs meanderingly through the middle of language, concealed and incomprehensible--and movable." However, because "someone or something has torn holes in [his] memory," he is completely unable to tell reality from fiction. When he reads Jan Wechsler's debut novel (the one that brought him into contact with Minsky in the first place), he recognizes bits of his own life in it and accuses the "other" Wechsler of the kind of theft Zichroni is guilty of: "This all feels like a conspiracy to me, as if the events are following a cleverly thought-out plot, designed to erase me, or at least my past, my identity, and my memory." It is for Wechsler as if someone else has painted his self onto the canvas that was rightfully his: "He had narrated *me*, without asking for my permission or even speaking to me."

Where Zichroni has access to others' memories, Wechsler doesn't even have access to his own. And yet he reaches many of the same conclusions as to the nature of memory and identity that Zichroni does. In a phrase that applies just as well to their linking character, Minsky, as to the two narrators, Wechsler says, "I am what I remember."[*]

The "I" seems to exist in *The Canvas* only insofar as it is continuous with past selves, and yet what it is at any given time but what it recalls? It exists with whatever memories it has, wherever they come from. What does this leave the reader but his (meaning my) interpretation of the story? The narrators versions of the events are at odds, and neither is to be trusted on its own, so where does the book have me come down? On the side of indeterminacy, on the side of flux. By assembling the book as he has, Stein forces the reader to participate in the story's telling, choosing, indeed, who gets to "tell" it first, who gets privileged. The two versions are themselves given to the reader (we do not read *ex nihilo*), but just introducing two options troubles the common relationship and calls into question the notion of an "official" text. *The Canvas* demonstrates, more clearly than most books, that there can ultimately be no mastery of a text.

And where does it leave me, The Synthesis, in thinking about my self apart from *this* book--an ambiguity here: this book, *The Canvas* but also this book, in vivo. If *The Canvas* teaches me that my self is my memories and I know that my memories are not mine but my author's, am I just a character in a book, like Zichroni, like Wechsler, like Minsky? I say *just* because the way it feels is I can be one thing and another. My author, Scott F. Parker, if he is himself a bundle of memories (some true, some false--truth, a falsity), is no different from me, except that he lives up in his head somewhere and I live down here on the page or the canvas, and once I'm recorded and the page

---

[*] Since Stein draws from "real life," he opens himself to the charge of being as guilty as his characters of stealing others' pasts. As guilty as Minsky and Wilkomirski of appropriating Holocaust trauma, as guilty as Zichroni's touch, as Wechsler's research?

is no longer blank my memories will stop changing
until someone comes with the eraser, the whiteout,
the computer virus, whatever--I might disappear,
I will disappear, but in the meantime I will not
change, as he will, his past rewritten . . . Except that in this book, this forward-facing book,
I have no past prior to my birth. I appear on the
page already walking, and if I need a past I will
invent it--or better, leave it unwritten--I too
will be an author. I am a fractured thing, broken
off in time. I have no memories because there ar-
en't any. And without memory, what is the self?

A more drastic scrambling even, Daniel Paul Schreber's *Memoirs of My Nervous Illness* ends before
it begins. Schreber offers his "remarks about the
nature of God and of the human soul" as axioms that
will be proved later. A proof, though, is only as
good as its axioms. Where are we? This tautology,
I'm curious where it leads, the process of becoming not undone as much as ongoing. Back to the beginning of the book, then, presumably, where the
end begins.*

If schizophrenia is a condition in which the
world is inside one's head, a schizophrenic book
might not be expected to correspond to what the
reader takes as the world. Whether the world is
everything that is the case (logic†) or everything

---

* Now I see that I'm in company, if not "sane" company, in
offering Weezy as if an axiom that my eventual proof will
necessitate. (Said another way: in Schreber, with Weezy, I
have synecdoches for in vivo itself.) Not that this is satisfactory, unless 1) we are bootstrapping Americans; 2) we are
satisfied Aristotelians (with The Synthesis the unmoved mover,
naturally); or 3) we abide in that not-yet-a-nothing. (*In and
as, a dream nowhere dreamed, the unmoved mover: all of us: no
us, just all.*)

† You know whose *Tractatus*, the line D. F. Wallace called one
of the two best first lines in the history of literature (or
something like that).

that's in one man's head (solipsism*), we can see
how much violence there is in knowing the way
things are. These are texts of mastery. How many
motherfuckers can say they psychotic?[†] How many of
us could if only we wanted to? "(The further content of this ~~chapter~~ paragraph is omitted as unfit
for publication.)"

But such violence occurs only external to the
subject, a subject that does not recognize any
external. In the closed system of a paranoid mind
there is only Truth, manifesting as Virtue. However, Schreber's megalomania admits of incomplete
sovereignty: "My nerves are influenced by the rays
to vibrate corresponding to certain human words;
their choice therefore is not subject to my own
will, but is due to an influence exerted on me from
without." Vibrations provide words in fragments
that the compulsive nerves "supplement to make up
the sense. It is in the nature of nerves that if
unconnected words or started phrases are thrown
into them, they automatically attempt to complete
them to finished thoughts satisfactory to the human
mind."

Schreber finds himself at the mercy of his mind,
which is at the mercy of external forces (the environment). If what a person is--or what a person
often thinks one to be--(without ever really admitting it) is what one thinks, then who one is
(in Schreber's model) is actually inseparable from
what one is not. Agency is almost a non-starter,
even for someone more powerful than God. Still the

---

* Our friend D. P. Schreber.
† M. Matthers asks this questions w/r/t schizophrenia, to
which I respond that I've never known someone with schizophrenia who was not working on a proof that he (from my experience) was at the center of some great understanding of how
everything fits together that no one else could appreciate. I
have also never not known myself to find this fascinating (and
envy it a little). So, schizophrenia, how many of us go it?
"You got it like I got it or not?"--no question.

noise comes in and you can listen to the noise or ignore the noise or talk over the noise but whatever response to the noise you make you respond to the noise. There is no not responding. Show me your power. When I was seven my nerves, too, heard noises when I would lie in bed at night unable to sleep . . . the noises were voices but the voices were without words or even a language--if it were light it would have been light from after the sunset when only the afterglow lingers before darkness comes--but it was not light, just sounds, and the sun had long since set, and only then did the sounds come alive, when the sun was down and the lights were out, emanating from just over some auditory horizon (the closest thing I can compare it to is the whispering from the first season of the television show Lost) . . . but the sounds were not sounds as much as energies that I chased around the room with my attention: I'd listen there in the room's upper left corner, but my ears were a beat slow and just as I heard from that corner the sound-energy would dart over there to the room's upper right corner, or the lower right, or the middle, or inevitably just above my face where if I stuck out my tongue maybe I could taste it . . . I did not never sleep . . . no, not never . . . those hours threatened to turn into years and they might have--they might, who knows, even still--but back then, thanks to something I figured out they did not: I realized that if I looked left and the energy went right, and if I looked right and the energy went left, I could influence, if not control, the location of the energy, and I could keep it away from me (I assumed it was dangerous--I was correct) by keeping my attention where I did not want to the energy to be (inside me)--and so I taught myself that year that even as I lay there in bed with the energy- sound in the room with me I could ignore it long enough that I could fall asleep. ¶ It was a different story when

I was twenty. A new energy appeared, this time from the inside--instead of coming for me it was coming from me. It was a harder energy to escape. Wherever I went there it already was. If the self is the stuff of conscious thought, then my self this time was large. The word should not precede consciousness (whose word would it be?) but it did, the word, so many words--all of them already coming from some wellspring long before there was anyone (I, namely) on the scene to receive them, no, to witness them coming and going--I was not myself the source, at least not volitionally--the words like great reams of prose being laid down inside me my mind, it felt, like there were pages and pages of words, the syntax dictating the content, the meaning that was incidental to the flow that we never be stopped or contained or even directed, just witnessed, ignored through occasional oblivion, but ever present, ever running, ever flowing, ever talking with my vocabulary, my sense of rhythm, my sense of what the world is and how it's connected to parts of itself and in and out of language and consciousness and thoughts and delusions and dreams--(are these dreams?)--and how it occurs in my bed where I'm trying to wake up and wondering how much I've missed already and when it will end and if I should write it down and how will my fingers ever move fast enough to capture it all--it all--there's so much of it and even if I am a mere stenographer I'll never lack for a sense of purpose...thereisworktobedone... thereisworktobedone... and if I cannot dictate it I can at least take the dictation . . .

So much comes back to sleep (so to speak), entering it and existing it. Schreber needs his sleep, too, but he's too "nervous" in much of his book to find it without drugs, ingested, internalized forces from the external. But the inability to sleep is due to an overstimulation of the nerves. How could the nerves not be over stimulated when, as he writes:

> I can put this point briefly: *everything that happens is in reference to me.* Writing this sentence, I am fully aware that other people may be tempted to think that I am pathologically conceited; I know very well that this very tendency to relate everything to oneself, to bring everything that happens into connection with one's own person, is a common phenomenon among mental patients. But in my case the very reverse obtains. Since God entered into nerve-contact with me exclusively, I became in a way for God the only human being, or simply the human being around whom everything turns, to whom everything that happens must be related and who therefore, from his own point of view, must also relate all things to himself.*

? And if a self moves in and out of a "nervous" state, can it be one thing and then not be that thing? What is it that moves? The selfsame noun? Without such continuity, what is the self?

---

* I'm reminded of Ram Dass, when he said that both the mystic and the schizophrenic say they're god, and it's only the schizophrenic who adds "and you're not."

CHAPTER 17: THE DISQUIET OF A TUMMY RUMBLING
[April 24, 3 a.m.]

Is it my stomach or my head? I believe certain
kinds of dinosaurs--sauropods--had two brains, one
in their heads, one above their tails. It must be
my stomach and my head. Though I still feel young
most days. I am in pain. I am not always in pain.
In fact, I'm so rarely in pain that fearing pain
becomes one of my great fears, which fear becomes
one of my great pains. But right now it's not as
complicated as all that. Right now: pain. Simple
pain. And my mind is swirling and what's the difference, I can't tell where one swirl stops and the
other starts. It's all swirly in here. I get up because I have to and wonder about ulcers and stress
because I don't know what else to wonder about.
Indigestion? Something else I've never had. Oh but
this is pain and yesterday was bloated, earlier
today it feels like. I started out mysteriously
hung over. After basketball the night before, I
had one beer while watching the NBA playoffs. I
had several glasses of water as well and the game
went into overtime. Overtime. Over time. What is
over time? What is under it. Nevertheless, I must
have been severely dehydrated and I woke up in the
morning feeling groggy with a headache unshakable.
[Nietzsche said style is everything--why does this
pop in my head now?] At 4, headache still present,
I had a beer with the gang after the Women in Publishing panel,* then a beer at 5 with F. and J. as
we do every week before Chekhov seminar, then at
10 another beer with S., O., and another J. to cel-

---

* About which, more soon.

ebrate S. passing her comprehensive exams for her
PhD. I expected the first one to function as a hair
of the dog, but shit there was no dog, I never got
bit, and I don't think any of it has anything to
do with why I'm hunched over massaging my stomach,
why I'm rolling around the bed waking up S., why
my dreams come in language instead of images or
narrative, spewing language never stopping never
started always just coming and overwhelming like a
drowning force--the first time I nearly drowned in
English was when I thought I was on the verge of a
schizophrenic break and could not decide whether
I wanted to step into that reality or hold back--
and the bitch of the thing was I knew, I knew, I
knew so bad, there was no way of deciding because
all my thoughts about deciding kept coming in English and were inseparable from the stream that
was being decided about, the decider was lost in
the material, a pattern that risked being lost in
the noise, and once I saw how easy it would be for
me to disappear into the noise, the chaos, I understood that I already had. And of course I was
nothing special, no one had ever un-disappeared,
yet I was the one up at night wishing for silence.
For silence. I must have found it because I don't
remember anyone asking me if I was as crazy as I
felt. No one noticed. So maybe I was fine. None of
which has anything to do with why I'm sitting on
the toilet chewing Tums and trying to shit my guts
out, why I'm so scared right now and more scared
that the scared will last. I know it won't, it never has before. Nevertheless: scared. Fuck you F.
Scott for being right about 3 a.m.

If I had to say why is why I'd say it's where
I live, in the space between everyone else where
enemies meet. I'm the medium the voices speak
through when they're almost communicating. I'm the
mirror you stare in when you ask yourself if you
like the look on your face, my taste is straight
reflection. The Synthesis cannot begin with this

because The Synthesis cannot begin, can only amal-
gamate. My voice becomes like a conversation heard
from a great distance, where there are no words
decipherable, only major themes. Representations,
representatives. Syn-the-sis, represent, represent. The Renegade here? The Renegade, hear? These
judgments, these propositions: synthetic a pos-
teri. I'm in the world. I'm in the streets (hall-
ways though they sometimes may be, tunnels). I'm
in the meeting. I'm sitting in every chair. My ass
is hard from sitting. And yet I'm standing up,
too. These fingers bleeding onto emails. I gather,
I gather, and try not to forget that I am a gath-
erer. I am a builder and I exhaust myself. I allow
myself to become exhausted.* But every so often my
powers return to me. How they do return! What I
learned by losing my mind was magic.

I started reading Pessoa last night and made
it as far as a few pages into Zenith's introduc-
tion and I'm in love. I'm in love with Pessoa, but
I'm more in love with what will come after: truth
and happiness and *Truth & Happiness*. I see it all
so clearly. There I am in a bungalow in Thailand
reading Proust, there I am with S. a few months
later on a beach in Malaysia deciding that what is
there to lose? There is literally nothing. I will
die and in the meantime I'd rather live with fear
than with regret. But there is fear and then there
is scared. I can't go on this way, terrified that
the pain will never end. But the pain will end and
I can go on forever. Everyone is crazy at 3 a.m.
We're just usually sedated. Sleep. Alcohol. TV

---

* More now. Yesterday was the Women in Publishing panel I
helped put on with money retrieved from a bureaucrat trying
to abscond. Politics. Everyone has an interest. Everyone has
feelings ready to be hurt. I just try to keep a level head
and make good decisions. But, as ever, I'd rather be alone in
some woods. Or with S. Yet, here is S., sleeping next to me
with a smile. And here I am lying awake experiencing pain.
It goes on and

binge. It's all the same. Except in that mad mani-
acal midnight when you're up so high you're sure
you can live right. I reside there or I reside in
silence, but for now I go on. I reside.

CHAPTER 18: ON THE MARGINS, CONT'D
[Disquiet - Silence]

The Book of Disquiet ends not in the middle, not before it begins, but never at all. Fernando Pessoa also is tired, this ongoing restless night, or in any case his semi-heteronym Bernando Soares is tired. "And now I'm sleepy, because I think--I don't know why--that the meaning of it all is to sleep." But short of sleeping, where we are afforded temporary reprieve from the burdens of consciousness,[*] when we are awake we must think and/or feel, dream and/or act, think or live. The logician in Pessoa/Soares understands that he has no ground to stand on in negotiating such binaries--even paralysis is merely one kind of action, one way that a person may (choose[†] to) live.[‡]

"To live is to not think."

Pessoa/Soares's narrator is one for whom instinct always leads toward the margin. He is inclined to think rather than feel or live and is therefore at a remove from what he identifies in lesser minds as *living*. Consistent with this disposition, he prefers to live remotely, from a place of observation vs. a place of participation (up there on the fourth floor above Rua dos Douradores). Encounters with the "other" seem to threaten the narrator's existence in his own private dreamscape (which might as well be interchangeable with reality). He prefers dreams and inaction to the limitation of

---

* "Life's basic malady, that of being conscious." & "I've always suffered more from my consciousness that I was suffering than from the suffering of which I was conscious."

† Though, like cats, we do not escape who or what we are.

‡ "Detesting both, I choose neither; but since I must on occasion either dream or act, I mix the two things together."

commitment. "Sympathy," for him, "leads to paralysis." Sympathy foregrounds the epistemological problems that plague this narrator. To decide anything is hard enough without taking into account the desires of multiple consciousnesses. One does not (cannot) know oneself well enough to act properly to achieve desired outcomes--how ever is one to know others well enough to promote their best ends? Better, this text argues, to remain neutral, passive, close as possible, if we will say so, to nonexistence.

In this attitude, Pessoa makes of himself a proto-existentialist: "I asked for very little from life . . . not to feel oppressed by the knowledge that I exist." Existence is a given in consciousness, but it is knowledge, not existence, that produces suffering. To not feel oppressed by it is either to not know it or to know it and not feel oppressed by it. The former comes with this blissful (and condescending) recommendation: "The truth isn't with him [the simple cook] or with me, because it isn't with anyone, but happiness does belong to him." The latter is an impossibility in Pessoa's strange and rainy Lisbon. To be self-aware is necessarily to suffer, and there is no enlargement of the self to transcendent levels that can sooth or satisfy that pain . . . except maybe in the freedom of dreams, where a conscious being might have access to perfection.

In waking life, the same problems occur (not that introducing problems to the story means they will be solved). Pessoa/Soares nostalgic. Not what once was. What once might have been. He dwells in perpetual possibility, where perfection continues to threaten paralysis. All action deviates from the perfection of dreams. A written text is never as good as an imagined one. A real life never as good as a dream.

Yet he writes. And in writing, he makes commitments: "I weep over my imperfect pages, but if future generations read them, they will be more touched by my weeping than by any perfection I might have achieved, since perfection would have kept me from weeping and, therefore, from writing. Perfection never materializes. The saint weeps, and is human. God is silent. That is why we can love the saint but cannot love God." Later, he explains: "In awe we worship the impulse to perfection of great artists. We love their approximation to perfection, but we love it because it is only an approximation."* As readers, we can come to love Pessoa/Soares for his repetitions, his obsession, his recursivity, his inability to end up anywhere but where he starts.† We can find, in short, perfection only in his idiosyncrasies (which is to say, his imperfections).

To memoir such a self--fictitiously, factlessly, (even sincerely?)--is to beg the question of the self itself. . . . In the writing that recounts the birth, it is born; without the writing, it never would have been there to begin writing. What came first, the memoir or the memoirist? "I gave birth to my infinite being, but I had to wrench myself out of me with forceps."

Reading Pessoa, what prevents the reader from throwing the book against the wall (or from hurling the lazy and common invective *navel-gazing* at him) is that he never assumes the self-importance of

---

* Perfection paralyses me. I prefer the messiness of imperfection because it is life--there is no room for purity--suicide is the only purity I recognize--the only logical conclusion: the only reason to survive: fuck logic, I will live live live. Despite it all, I will live live live. Art is not perfect, to perfect art is to perfect its imperfections. To return to some earlier examples: the nonsense of Wayne; Dylan's "all the notes are in there" singing; the cuteness of Derrida. And then of course, too: the arbitrary sprawliness of Pessoa, the limitations of The Synthesis. *Homo sum, humani nihil a me alienum puto. Memento mori.*

† "And I ~~stop~~ start writing because I ~~stop~~ start writing." (corrected by The Synthesis)

which Kierkegaard accused Hegel.* *The Book of Disquiet* will never represent a system (for Pessoa) because it will never be complete (for Pessoa) nor perfect: "And I, whose self-critical spirit allows me only to see my lapses and defects, I, who dare write only passages, fragments, excerpts of the non- existent, I myself--in the little that I write--am also imperfect."

On becoming a(n incomplete) book: "I am, in large measure, the selfsame prose I write." And this is an ironic, which is to say hypothetical, project. If, as Pessoa/Soares says, "All literature is an attempt to make life real," then what is made real in a literature that presents itself as a dream? A dream of a dream. Literature is an attempt, not a fact. And the consciousness that produces literature, or any work of art, is limited, and is always relational and disposed to go meta: "Since we can't extract beauty from life, let's at least try to extract beauty from not being able to extract beauty from life. Let's make our failure into a victory, into something positive and lofty, endowed with columns, majesty and our mind's consent."†

Where could a man such as this live but in a

----

* "If Hegel had written the whole of his logic and then said, in the preface or some other place, that it was merely an experiment in thought in which he had even begged the question in many places, then he would certainly have been the greatest thinker who had ever lived. As it is, he is merely comic."
† A note on originality: Reading Pessoa as The Synthesis, I keep seeing my own thoughts returned back to me in Emersonian fashion. My genius was to born with the philosopher the day after tomorrow, the world as my witness. But I'm not holding back. I too

enjoy being here

wherever this is

& even if

I don't know what to take

when I go

vortex. Well? "Yes, for me the Rua dos Douradores contains the meaning of everything and the answer to all riddles, except for the riddle of why riddles exist, which can never be answered." Perhaps we are all in this vortex tasked with the impossible task to: move! act! live! *But how*, we either ask or do not ask.

If no way is in itself the best (*best* would be in reference to exactly what?), then action, paralysis, and writing are equally viable--what's not is the sincerity or faith that one's response to our condition is any more than this. And so Pessoa/Soares: "I *indifferently* narrate my factless autobiography, my lifeless history. These are my Confessions, and if in them I say nothing, it's because I have nothing to say" (emphasis mine). And if it is written (it is written), how do we read it? Again: "To read is to dream, guided by someone else's hand. To read carelessly and distractedly is to let go of that hand. To be only superficially learned is the best way to read well and be profound." I am profoundly validated. It was written.

Not who am I but what am I?

"Who am I to myself? Just one of my sensations." If the self is just one of one's sensations and sensations are in flux then the self, too, is in flux, which is to say a multitude. An author of a self, then, less an omniscient creator than a well-meaning recorder. There may be conclusions here, but finding them would require a conclusive thinker--someone outside or otherwise without a self. It won't be Pessoa.[*] No, the recorder influences, shapes, creates (partially), and in all

---

[*] "In these considerations there may be an entire philosophy for someone with the strength to draw conclusions. It won't be me."

"There are days that are philosophies, that suggest interpretations of life, that are marginal notes--full of critical observations--in the book of our universal destiny."

other ways *participates*, but he does not *know*: "Not even I know if this I that I'm disclosing to you, in these meandering pages, actually exists or is but a fictitious, aesthetic concept I've made of myself." The self that a memoirist writes is based on the one s/he is given. For Pessoa/ Soares: "I have to say what I feel, given that I'm I." The givenness of this "I" is only apparent. What if I'm not I--what if I'm not-I? Sensations, like concepts, sometimes fold in on themselves and vanish. The whole becomes a hole. As in: "Today I was struck by an absurd but valid sensation. I realized, in an inner flash, that I'm no one. Absolutely no one." Without an "I," what is the self?

To repeat: Without memory, what is the self? Without continuity, what is the self? Without an "I," what is the self? If the self is fractured, was it at one time not fractured? Could it be the fracture itself--and then is a fracture a thing or a place where a thing ceases to be a thing? These are simple questions. Please find answers in the footnote following the completion of this sentence.*

To repeat: Moving on. The fractured selves of *The Canvas, Memoirs of My Nervous Illness*, and *The Book of Disquiet* are dramatized by their respective narratives' various fictions. Even so, each employs the assumed reality of the self as a being while troubling/complicating/challenging it. The narrative "I" speaks on behalf of some entity, whether this entity is real, imaginary, grammatical necessity, or a way of passing the time. Even Pessoa, whose narrator writes himself into being, reaches only for the present moment,† coming to terms with now but leaving forever to grasp after

---

*

† Though in reaching for the present, he already faces an impossible task: his present retreats as fast as he approaches it in an infinite series of moments reaching out into the future.

"From so much self-thinking, I'm now my thoughts and not I."

itself. The present _in vivo_ pursues is not the one that's always just getting away but the one that never seems like it's getting any closer. The turning point of a memoir is often the key moment when that "I" turned into _this one_. But in the case where that "I" is ahead not being and will never arrive, whether or not there's one here to begin with, what does it mean to memoir? Let us keep trying to recall the future.

If someone (and for now let's say it's me) were to invert the time with which a memoir were interested, would it not also make sense to invert the page on which the memoir were composed,

would it not be natural for the text to move into the margins as the author explores the idea that that there is no such thing as a "marginal" text, that any so-called "main" text is only the margin to some "other" text in an ongoing shifting of contexts. The turning point for such a text would not be in any realization, but rather in the putting into practice. The "turning point" that maybe there are no "margins," that all surfaces are possible sites for text, on which a self might be self-consciously written, produced-- would be the performance of form inseparable from content--the project of inventing the future taken up not by the author whose control over the text reaches its limit[*] at the asymptotic present but by the reader who collaborates in the creation of a communication. Without a reader there is no writ-

---

[*] Literally.

ing. The untold story (and all unheard stories are untold) is too perfect to register. If I'm going to exist, I must register. If I'm going to exist, I require proof. If I'm going to exist. If . . . . .

"The only noble destiny for a writer who publishes is to be denied a celebrity he deserves," writes Pessoa's narrator, whose celebrated text denies its author the anonymity he does not deserve. "But the truly noble destiny belongs to the writer who doesn't publish. Not who doesn't write, for then he wouldn't be a writer. I mean the writer in whose nature it is to write, but whose spiritual temperament prevents him from showing what he writes." To overflow oneself and to ask no one else to share the burden.* One thinks here of Nietzsche--who one often thinks of, reading Pessoa--when he admitted:

> But why do you write? --A: I am not one of those who think with an inky pen in their hand, much less one of those who in front of an open inkwell abandon themselves to their passions while they sit in a chair and stare at the paper. I am annoyed by and ashamed of my writing; writing is for me a pressing and embarrassing need, and to speak of it even in a parable disgusts me.
>
> B: But why, then, do you write? --A: Well, my friend, to be quite frank: so far, I have not discovered any other way of getting rid of my thoughts. --B: And why do you want to get rid of them? --A: Why I want to? Do I want to? I must. --B: Enough! Enough!

"So why do I [Pessoa/Soares] keep writing? Because I haven't learned to practise completely the renunciation that I preach." And I? I efface such

----

* A burden--the burden of consciousness--that cannot be shared. Each of us is alone in this . . .

rational personal issues. The Synthesis writes for publication because he doesn't know what else to do. Without writing he would not exist and he would rather exist than not, so he writes himself. Call him a coward, for a coward he is.[*] Standing over the void, suspended between being and nonbeing, trying not to look down, trying not to blink, trying only to maintain constant and perfect focus. But for him to exist he must accept, no, embrace, no, love imperfection. The void itself is perfect, the void itself is purity, the void itself is death. Between being and nonbeing there is a non. Anon: walk the imperfect path--you cannot love purity without falling in, and when you fall into a pit with no bottom you quickly acclimate and fail to appreciate that you are, indeed--but be sure that you are--falling. Falling. And, depending on your disposition, maybe taking notes as well on the way down. Thus spake The Synthesis.[†]

Without □ , what is the self? Without □ , what is
Without □ , what is the self? Without □ , what is t
Without □ , what is the self? Without □ , what is the
Without □ , what is the self? Without □ , what is the se
Without □ , what is the self? Without □ , what is the self?
Without □ , what is the self? Without □ , what is the self? Wit
Without □ , what is the self? Without □ , what is the self? Without
Without □ , what is the self? Without □ , what is the self? Without □ ,
Without □ , what is the self? Without □ , what is the self? Without □ , what
Without □ , what is the self? Without □ , what is the self? Without □ , what is the
Without □ , what is the self? Without □ , what is the self? Without □ , what is the self?
Without □ , what is the self? Without □ , what is the self? Without □ , what is the self? Without
Without □ , what is the self? Without □ , what is the self? Without □ , what is the self? Without □ , what i
Without □ , what is the self? Without □ , what is the self? Without □ , what is the self? Without □ , what is the self?
Without □ , what is the self? Without □ , what is the self? Without □ , what is the self? Without □ , what is the self? Without □ , wha
Without □ , what is the self? Without □ , what is the self? Without □ , what is the self? Without □ , what is the self? Without □ , what is the self? With

Non-Errata:

the phrase 'Pessoa/Soares nostalgic' on page so-and-so, is correct as is, with the subject taking

---

[*] Pessoa agrees: "This book is my cowardice. . . .Writing is like the drug I abhor and keep taking, the addiction I despise and depend on."

[†] Classmate: So, what did she think?

*no action--(aha! the fragment of inaction!) But
what does this have to do with what I was thinking? Nothing, which is why I let myself think it.**

---

* Hear the disquiet here.

CHAPTER 19: ON HEARING
[SILENCE - SOUND]

How about a joke in which the punch line
is never delivered, or a game

in which the goalposts are moved
just beyond comprehension--

and we agree to keep playing?
There are so many ways to build a fire.

The language that gets most quickly to
silence would be the language that

would be the language that
would be the language that

would be the language that
. . . (I assure you this is

no printer's error, these marks, and
there is no danger in running out

of stories to tell.)

CHAPTER 20: FICTITIOUS WORLDS
[Fictitious Times]

In the Chekhov seminar F., J., and I are in, Professor L. has offered to let the three of us turn
in short stories (w/ Chekhov-related expositions)
for our final projects instead of the fifteen-page
critical papers he's requiring from the other
graduate students. This generous offer stares at
me like the curse of getting what I want. Looking
for the easy way out, now I must face the fact that
my interest in writing a critical paper on Chekhov
is underdone only by my comfort writing fiction.
   Stalling on the story one day in the library, I
email F., who writes fiction with seeming ("!" she
might say) ease to ask some important questions
such as: How many words is it good to use in a story? And what's a good name for a woman who is both
old and proficient with computers? She responds: "I
use 1800 words. J. uses 9000. You can fit anywhere
in that range. Good names are: Berta, Stefanie,
Miriam." Now I have something to go on.
   The story I'm trying to write has something
to do with a comment L. made in class one week
about how in Tolstoy's "Death of Ivan Illych," the
eponymous protagonist is able to face death with
equanimity because of his faith, whereas in Check-
hov's "Dreary Story" the protagonist isn't granted
that comfort. The question I wanted to explore was
what it would take and what it would look like for
someone to face death with Illych's equanimity but
without his faith. The idea probably attracted me
because someone close to me died recently and I
was thinking about his degree of inner peace and

where it came from. I will resist the temptation here to digress and stick instead to how the fiction writing goes.

It goes like this: Some moments I feel like I'm trapped in a little tiny box. Then there seem to be moments when the walls fall down and maybe were never there. I go back and forth, overwhelmed by all the directions things can move.

I get up from my corral at the library and go looking for "Ivan Illych," which I'm pretty sure I read once ten years ago. An eerie moment follows when I sit back down with a disintegrating copy of Tolstoy's stories. I can't tell if I have read the story before or not, but there's something very familiar about this story I'm trying to write. It isn't deja vu but a memory I can't quite access.

Then it hits me that I have written fiction before. Fiction based on Tolstoy. Ten, eleven years ago. I was in college at the time, reading Tolstoy's *Confessions* and I wrote a story in which a character sits in a coffee shop reading that book again and again in a version she abridged herself, excising everything after the Christian conversion. It occurs to me that this is a wonderful excuse to take a break from writing and go searching through my hard drive and email archives and various clouds until I find "No Confession Necessary," a first-person story told by a Schopenhauer-inspired narrator who has just been killed stepping into traffic in a quasi-suicide. Reading it now I am reminded how earnest I was (has anything changed?), how serious I could be (has anything changed?), how necessary it felt to build an intellectual foundation to life (has anything changed?), how I was trying to use persona and ironic distance to tell the story I wanted to tell without having to "tell" it (has anything changed?). Has *anything* changed?

I continue wandering through the clouds, now searching to see if there were other stories left up there. Lo and behold, there are several, including one about a breakup, one about a mushroom trip, and one with a stoned narrator dictating his thoughts into a tape recorder. These stories are like foreign artifacts or memories from someone else's life, but as I read through them I start to feel myself staking a claim to them. The more of them I read the more the stranger's history starts to become mine. This stranger—this writer—must have lived in some dark corner inside me, somewhere behind my eyes where I could not see. Besides the stories, I find essays, poems, letters, rants. It makes me wonder how I possibly wrote so much without noticing it. Was I always a writer—one who for a long time failed to realize it?

There's more material here than I could possibly read before the library closes. But even without rereading all of it I can see that I've discovered in this old work one of the things in vivo is about: reading brings me closer to the younger self taking shape in my mind. I have sympathy for him, respect for what he was trying to do. I hope I'm living up to the plans he had for me. I want to reach back and tell him it's OK, and I think he's trying to tell me the same thing. Why else would he have left so many clues? But I can't reach him. All I can do is repeat the gesture by trying to reach out to . . .

CHAPTER 21: ON THE REAL
[becoming less relevant...or more subjective...]

There's one more story I found in the cloud that is staying on my . . . "Never Mind" features a character, Scott, giving a presentation on quantum metaphysics--his idea that observation more than determines, actually creates, reality. Effectively, he's making an argument for idealism that encounters the challenge of having to account for the existence of a subjectivity that accounts for the collapse of the initial wave function. What's interesting, if not very successful, is how the text engages this idea formally. The author interrupts the scene of the presentation to point out that if Scott's interpretation were true (for flawed reasoning, I might add) reality itself would fade out of existence. As the interruption is being made, it begins to . . .
    I'm thinking of that story now for two reasons. 1) Because I'm reading a new popular physics book that seems to jibe (at least loosely) with the story's presentation's and performance's thesis. 2) Because the presenter's theory of quantum metaphysics seems to be of a piece with the project of in vivo. [Is it possible to read "Never Mind" as the ur-text for The Synthesis?*]
    1) A sample of notes scribbled while reading popular physics book:

----
* Maybe it is. I begat/bootstrapped myself only a month or so later when I started writing *Introducing The Synthesis*, the first of my two a cappella rap albums. I wrote that album, you heard, because I felt compelled to exist. And I did. I felt compelled to exist because that's how I compelled myself to feel. Tell me a better origin story than that.

- some "event" described from various partici-
  pants' PsOV--there's no objective position,
  narrative presence, just whatever comes of
  the sum
- if solipsism is the way things "really are"
  our experience continues to be at odds with
  it
- no outside (math, universe, reality, text)
  no margins, only thing itself----we are the
  mirror----
- observer's collapse=collapse for that observ-
  er--that's so crazy! final blow to "reality"
- on the other hand, so obvious. how does the
  observer (the original one) appear in the first
  place to collapse the wave function (the original)*--it doesn't have to . . . i (every "i")
  am not a destiny, i am a possibility . . .†
- if you are it, it disappears
  whatever it is
  there is no self-referentiality
  be the place from which . . .
  there is nothing outside the light

2) in vivo takes a different angle of approach.
The major implicit fear stemming from the above
is that the world becomes (always was?) no bigger
than our ideas of it. This is the loneliest and
saddest thought I can imagine. I'd like to look for
a trapdoor through which I could escape by having
an idea of a world that is bigger than any world
limited by my ideas.‡ Wittgenstein once said, "The

---

* Returns me to "Never Mind."
† I can't say exactly what this means, but I can tell I
thought it was profound when I recorded it--and I think it
might be profound, if only I could understand it
‡ While I do not think I'm smart enough to trick myself in
this regard, I take solace from the Hindu idea that existence

subject does not belong to the world." Before him, Emerson said, "All is a riddle, and the key to a riddle . . . is another riddle."

in vivo tries to create the future--or at least narrate its coming into being--and this future is a world, a world that is constantly expanding to contain the ever-expanding past, every idea upon idea, every set of all sets becoming merely one part of the next set of all sets, *ad . . . ad . . . ad infin*--yet as this world expands so too it shrinks. As we know well: the child's world is so much larger than the adult's precisely because it's so much smaller.

So why not just get lost in abstraction? There's no reason not to. *Not that I can think of.* Get it? Not that I can think of. Hegel. Emerson. Nietzsche. Proust. Wittgenstein. 2Pac. Karl Ove Knausgaard. Fuck you. The Synthesis. What's wrong with "the way things are"?

Allow me to state my concerns.

If solipsism is a fact, is it still solipsism?
Is finding solipsism an unfortunate outcome enough to preclude it?
Limits are everything. Literally.*

---

is a drama the divine performs for itself--and that the most important part of the performance is to forget it's a performance.
* And do they exist?

CHAPTER 22: PRESENTING MY I
[MAY 15, 2014, 9:00 AM]*

My "I"
Begging the Question of Self in Creative Nonfiction

0. Play "Jokerman" video.

1. Thanks for coming to this early morning session. Special thanks to V., B., and F., who were with me the day I started to think about this book (at Stub & Herb's, I believe), and have been with me every day since. Thanks to S. who, among much other wise council these past few years, a time when I've certainly needed it, made me throw out my presentation two days ago and start from scratch. Also special thanks to J., without whom there wouldn't be donuts.

2. The title of my presentation is [SLIDE] and

---

* Before the presentation, I wake up early and go for a run around Lake of the Isles, then I shower, dress, and ride my bike to campus. I'm still an hour early but not as nervous as I might have expected. Before before, like earlier this week, S. looked at a draft of the talk for my presentation and made me throw it out and start over. The topic was fine, she said, but the approach was all off. Thinking back to the conversation with B. and F. at Common Roots a couple months back, I had written a narrative of how the thesis had come to be as a way of reflecting on the "I" in nonfiction. S.'s feedback was that while it was fine to talk about what I wanted to talk about (vs. whatever I imagined was expected of me), explaining that decision in the talk, rather than just doing it, put me on the defensive. Like I was justifying my claim instead of staking it. This particular interrogation of the "I" might have grown out of in vivo, but it can be applied just fine to any nonfiction work.

since I've got my Scott F. Parker mask on we're
ready to get started.

I. What even is it?

Today I was struck by an absurd but
valid sensation. I realized, in an inner
flash, that I'm no one. Absolutely no one.
--Pessoa

3. As readers, when we meet "I" on the page of a
work of nonfiction, we meet a stranger. This lonely pronoun stands for nothing and as nothing but
a promise of future intimacy. For writers, the
experience can feel nearly the inverse. "I" is
the word we assume we know best, the word through
which all others are known to us, the word through
which language and communication become possible.

4. Beginning writers, ensconced in their own private "I"s or urges toward self-expression often
forget how much the reader knows (nothing) and
needs to be told (everything--or everything relevant, anyway). And so we have the sound nonfic-
tion-writing advice to *introduce* the "I." If readers get all or enough relevant attributes they
will know the particular person the "I" stands
for, is the idea. And to the extent that readers
are looking for working characters on the page,
this will do. An individuated "I," versus some
vague and distant pronoun, is one you might enjoy
the company of and want to spend your reading time
with.

5. I think it gets more complicated when we reflect
on the assumption in nonfiction that the "I" on the
page refers to something more substantial off it--
namely the self that floats mysteriously somewhere
between your ears and behind your eyes. (If we
wanted to lump nonfiction in with fiction, we could

stop right here, and deny any signification of the "real," but I don't think that's something most of us want to do.) The "non-" of nonfiction is often central to why we read it. However, if we read with the assumption that the word "I" corresponds with a unique and individual person going around the world thinking, acting, experiencing, the question I want to ask is: Does it?

6. I want to suggest that the self, as we usually know it, is a naive concept. For practical reasons we rely on it. It helps us communicate, organize experience, navigate the world. Without it we'd be, well, lost, undifferentiated from our environments. In a very real sense, without a private and personal interiority I-- "I"--can't be said to exist. Yet we know this interior space only through a one-way window, only until the very moment we try to bring it into consciousness awareness, then suddenly it's nowhere to be found. We become like knives thinking we could cut ourselves if only we were a little sharper or moved a bit more swiftly. The "I" arises in the gap between observer and observation. This subject exists only in distinction from its objects. And anything the "I" can observe is necessarily not-"I."

7. Think again about that instruction we give nonfiction writers to *introduce* the "I," but this time keep in mind Hume's famous passage from *A Treatise on Human Nature*: [SLIDE] "For my part, when I enter most intimately into what I call *myself*, I always stumble on some particular perception or other, of heat or cold, light or shade, love or hatred, pain or pleasure. I never can catch *myself* at any time without a perception and never can observe anything but the perception. When my perceptions are removed for any time, as by sound sleep, so long am I insensible of myself and may truly be said not to exist."

8. Sri Ramana Maharshi, the Indian guru of last century, would have agreed with Hume that what we normally call the self is fleeting, but he goes on to offer a positive (if radically counterintuitive) definition of the self as that which is present in deep dreamless sleep.

9. For another approach we might think of the negative theology of the Upanishads: *neti, neti*. The self, or Atman, is Brahman, but Brahman is not this, not this. Which makes it . . . what? If we take a step back from the qualia of experience (whether Hume's step or Ramana's), who or what, then, is left to do the experiencing? And so on, ad infinitum. What is it that we actually want our nonfiction writers to introduce?

10. This is the moment I could invite you to join me in a meditation and this whole presentation could take a really weird turn, but I think art (including, I guess, presentations) works better when it satisfies itself with raising questions. So instead of telling you where I think this leads metaphysically, I'll to turn to writing and how I think it can and does illuminate and provoke the issue.

II. Writing as a kind of performance.

I will also essay to be.
--Emerson

11. As the other nonfiction writers here will tell you, we get asked sometimes why we write nonfiction. (Realistically, though, we're more likely to be asked what "creative nonfiction" even is.) What I usually say (to the first question) is that nonfiction affords the writer the chance to think on the page, and it offers the reader the chance (to paraphrase Virginia Woolf) to be drawn inside

the curtain of another person's consciousness. It is--or at least it can be--a deeply intimate and empathic encounter. Rarely in our time, if in any, do we get the opportunity to share such proximity with others.

12. Given this interest on my part, it doesn't so much matter for me the subject matter of a work of nonfiction. While it's true I'd read just about any-one writing on Dylan, it's a more meaningful truth that I'll read, for example, Zadie Smith writing on anything. I enjoy spending readerly time with the consciousness she creates and shares on the page.

13. To clarify here, the question I'm raising is not the question of fiction, whether Smith in real life is like the Smith whose mind we encounter on the page. In fact, I assume with all writers that their nonfiction personae are better people than their authors: smarter, funnier, more compas-sionate, more generous. (Although, I need to add, thanks to Terri Sutton, I got to be Smith's escort when she was here last fall and she was very cool in person too.)

14. Remaining, though, is the question of what's being constructed. It might be a better self, but we still have to ask: what's one of those? As with the ontological "I," I think the written "I" works most easily when we accept it naively. When we look too deeply into any word--not just "I"--it begins to bend under our attention, becoming diffi-cult to define, to use, to make meaning from. Con-ceptually, it becomes inseparable from its nega-tion. The world of chairs depends entirely on the world of not-chairs. Just as well, it depends on definition and use. Must it have four legs? If not, is being used for sitting enough to make something a chair? (What about those giant Adirondack chairs that people in Minnesota for some reason have in

their yards?) And so on. Meaning depends entirely on making an infinite number of convenient approximations.

15. OK, so, words don't map neatly onto so-called reality, language isn't innocent. What I think makes this *interesting*, with respect to the "I" is that (unlike, usually, in day-to-day life) on the page we can *productively* interrogate the self, especially in nonfiction writing. And not only as a byproduct of the text (though definitely that) but also as a central feature of the text. What's wonderful about creative nonfiction is that as soon as you develop the least bit of sophistication as a reader, you stop seeing the "I" as a given, as you must in fiction, where--precisely because it's fiction--the text cannot lie. The construction, then, of the self becomes one of the main subjects (if you will) of the text. We enter a veritable hall of mirrors. Some author is presenting some version of himself in such a way that you, the reader, will perceive him as he wants to be perceived (or so he tries). It's not a big leap to see that the self he performs for you draws from the one he performs for himself--and he is, as you are, on uncertain ground.

16. Often, the best nonfiction (in my opinion) will forefront the tangle and complexity of selfhood such that the construction and performance of self becomes a focus of the prose. Examples here include: Pessoa, Emerson, Montaigne, Didion, Zadie Smith again, Eula Biss, not to mention pretty much every decent memoir ever written.

17. The example I want to spend a few minutes thinking about, though, is Dylan. And not Dylan the memoirist, though he is a good one, but Dylan as he performs himself as a public concept. And I want to do so by looking at his Cadillac commer-

cial from this year's Super Bowl.

18. A week or two after that first aired, I was at the bar with a couple of friends and it came up in conversation. They each accused Dylan of selling out, and had the ad featured another financially successful artist I might have been quick to agree with them. But with Dylan, I speculated, the concept of selling out doesn't really apply. Did he sell out when he started turning from rock 'n' roll to folk music right here in Dinkytown? Did going back to electric in fact make him a Judas? Who or what was he selling out when he went country? When he isolated himself with his family on their farm? When he became a Christian fundamentalist? When he made a Christmas album? Each time, and dozens of others, he was accused of selling out. Which Dylan should we call the real Dylan? Typically, I'm afraid, for most people it's whichever one happens to be their personal favorite that they call real. As Cate Blanchett says, playing a version of Dylan in the aptly titled *I'm Not There*, "You only want me to say what you want me to say." If there's one thing we know by now not to expect from Dylan, it's that. So one way of looking at this is that he is constantly selling himself out. My way of looking at it, though, is that Dylan's performance of so many selves hollows out the concept of an essential self. What makes Dylan's case interesting is not that he's uniquely malleable but that he's uniquely public in his performance of malleability. (I want to emphasize, though, that I'm not endorsing this commercial.)

III. How did "I" get here?

He beat the drum of freedom, pretty much all the time. His message was to be as big as you have it in you to be.
--Sunshine Kesey

19. Analogous to Dylan's various incarnations are the various forms of writing and uses of "I" employed in my essay collection *How Big the Bigness Is*. The book combines memoir, travel writing, nature writing, literary criticism, and prose poetry. What, if anything, holds them together in one unified work?

20. The typical answer to this question I think would be that it's the underlying consciousness of the author that holds the various selves in common. Think of Whitman's multitudes. He *contains* them. But I hope I've sufficiently troubled the concept of a unified self (however many selves it might contain) that I need to produce a different answer. And in fact, searching for such an answer was one of the major challenges in assembling this book. In terms of craft, I can say that the text dramatizes the relationship between self and environment through its deployment of form. I've frontloaded the more memoiristic pieces to introduce the narrator and to allow the book's organization to reproduce structurally its main argument that a subject can exist only in relation to its environment. As the book proceeds, the "I" is de-emphasized vis-a-vis stuff like trees, cougars, and the plastic we find washed up on the beach. But the craft question wasn't quite the one I was really interested in. Then, one morning this spring, during a dharma talk given by Steve Hagen [aside here depending on time?], I figured out what it was I'd been doing all along.

21. What Hagen said that struck me was that if there were a reason to meditate he wouldn't do it. If it were for the sake of enlightenment or to calm his emotions or lower his blood pressure or whatever, he wouldn't do it. Meditation would be just one more mean to one more end. It is the utter pur-

poselessness of meditation that makes it valuable and worthwhile for him. Why did I write this book? For the same reason I go running around the lakes, which is no reason at all. If I can offer a tautology that I hope is more meaningful to you than Dylan's "America is America," I wrote this book because I wrote *this* book. I wrote it because it is play. Even if there's no one doing the playing.

22. And now to transition into what I'm going to read, which is from the title essay about Ken Kesey, here's a synchronistic quote from a lecture Kesey gave in '65 right about the time he was quitting writing: "When you run across someone who is writing for entirely selfish reasons because it's what he wants to do, you get something where you begin to feel the contact. Even though you may not understand it. Bob Dylan is the best example that I can explain right now."

23. That's more than a lot for me to live up to, but here's how big the bigness is:

CHAPTER 23: ANY QUESTIONS?
[AFTERWARD/AFTERWORD]

What happened to V. & A. & the others? We *know,*
obviously, but readers will be curious. And what
about the fears and excitement they provoked in
The Synthesis?

Early on in the project, S. was reminding me to
come back to the ground and not float too far away.
Inevitably, though, I floated and left the story
and the time-structure behind. Thanks for reminding me.
    V., B., and F. wrote and presented their theses
as predicted in the text. I'll leave it to them to
describe their emotions vis-à-vis the experience;
mine is relief that it's over.
    A. is healthy and thriving.
    All parties continue to see one another fre-
quently.

How do you feel now that the option to drop out is
officially no longer an option?

Definitely some embarrassment. I'll never be able
to be a writer who does not have an MFA. It's a
fact I have to get used to carrying around with
me. Luckily, most people have never heard of an
MFA and wouldn't even know where to begin caring
whether someone has one.
    As the self expands through time and contains
more past selves within, it also shrinks in rela-

---

* All Qs by F. and B., who have provided them after reading
the manuscript through this point.

tion to all the potential selves history cuts it off from. Life, increasingly, becomes a necessity more than a possibility. I can never *remain* this self, but the number of selves I can never *be* expands exponentially.

Is it possible to please a self that you write / produce / publish? (p. 109)

I'm not at all sure pleasing is what we should hope for our selves. Not because--to answer your question--it's not possible but because of the ways in which it's not possible. Since you ask this in reference to p. 109, when I go back and read that page what I see is an "I" that knows it can't win but lacks the ethical creativity to locate viable alternatives to its existential dread. That "I"'s version of checking his phone to see if he's alive is checking his Amazon sales rank to see if he's really a writer, as if book sales = writing and writing is something > writing. The inadequacy this kind of thinking suggests is a hole that will never be filled, a black hole of self that expands the more that's put into it.

Do you write to be seen? Or is being seen a face-pinking bi-product of writing to be _____?

This is a hard-hitting and critical question for me. Of course, writing is a way to be seen without being seen, a way of existing in the world without having to be there too, a way in other words of being in multiple places at once or of leaving little traces to do my work for me. Let's keep trying: a way to be present while absent as a response to feelings of sometimes being absent while present. There's part of me that likes to hide in public. There's part of me that wants to be well known *so that* I can become a recluse. So that's part of the story anyway, the desperate part, psychic urges that undoubtedly have their causes.

But there's another part of the story about someone who writes only to be read and would be happy to be anonymous (or heteronymous?). He is the reader, first, who has been helped so much by the written word that he can't help but want to return the favor. Helped in the sense of getting to know the world and how people experience and have experienced it. It's that mysterious consolation that one (and one's perspective) is never complete (meaning one is never ultimately alone)--there is always some other way of seeing things (and/or way of seeing new things). In particular, he is interested in people's lives, how they live them, what they learn from them. Memoir for him is a distinctly ethical form. He wants to hear their confessions, their revelations; and therefore he too must confess, reveal. If being revealed is a consequence of constantly revealing, so be it.

Did you grow up reading the Bible?

I was not raised that way. However, I was around it enough to occasionally become curious and look at different parts of it. I was probably finished growing "up" by the time I got into the Gnostic Gospels, which taught me most of what I understand about politics, history, and contingency.

Going back to Augustine, memoir usually employs an "I-now" reflecting on an "I-then." Is in vivo all "I-now" or is there an "I-then" lurking somewhere?

I'm inclined first of all to say it's all "I-now" except that isn't true anymore. The "I-now" that exists in the narration of memoir exists in the perpetual present moment of the text. It is in other words an effect *produced* by the text, by a reading of the text. As long as there is a reader there is a creation of the now. But in vivo means to complicate this relationship further by denying the possibility of a cohesive now from which the narration occurs. The limited perspective of the narrator produces a temporal conflation of "I-now" and "I-then" that is simultaneously both entirely the former and entirely the latter. At the moment of composition, I is all now. But each successive "I-now" is made "I-then" by the ongoing unfolding of the composition. Each chapter's "I" includes the previous chapter's "I," which includes . . . and it goes on like this in Russian- doll fashion.

What in vivo really denies is the privileging of some ultimate "I." There is no God's-I view here. Even now as I adopt this tone of knowingness, I am aware that the book is yet to reach its conclusion and that even after it does reach its conclusion it will not be completed, only abandoned, as Leonardo said.

The place I'd like to get to is where the mirror can reflect itself. I don't know where the light would get in, but if it did, boy, would it shine.

Re: blogs, diaries, archives: what's in between public and private?

My hunch is to say everything. Or everything good, anyway.

I count myself among those writers who think that one of the things that make literature/art special is that it/they can connect otherwise isolated individuals. Reading (something I love) has always been a deeply intimate experience for me. But public/private: one of the things about that connection is the bridging but not conflating of the two. It's not that the private is or is made public, it's that the private is accessible publicly. So to me it's more about the accessing than what's accessed. I used to push this theory that because memoir is primarily about its method a bad memoir is as valuable to read as a good one.

I've read too many bad memoirs now to really hang
onto this idea, but I'd to retain a weaker version
of the claim. Even a bad memoir, *in its way of
telling*, reveals its author's self-understanding,
which is memoir's prime directive: to fix the
self in time.

You know a bad memoir when you feel pity for
the author, when you assess his or her self-understanding and find it impoverished. At its bone,
memoir is an ethical form, and it's ethical in two
ways: first, empathetically--we see through someone else's eyes; and second, literally so--we are
offered alternatives approaches to the project of
living. The first is foundational to the second as
well as to the form itself. We feel in and then
assess the wisdom there. Does it fit us? This memoir that was written as if for me at twenty, does
my self still read its higher aims in it? If not,
what or who am I looking for now? I keep reading.

Memoirists must be as honest as possible on
the page (not about what happened--though that
too--as much as what it's like to be alive) and
not for their own sake but for the reader's. Diaries, however, can be cathartic/therapeutic, they
can be documentary, they can be sincerely private
but only if you never die or develop some kind of
method to keep them secret when you do. They're
private even when they're public. The reader is a
voyeur. Blogs, though, are public even when no one
reads them. When that tree falls it goes on making
a sound whenever someone's there to hear it. One
thing that's fun, of course, is intentionally dis-
rupting the two: diaries that are written for the
eventual other and public writing that exposes the
private. In either case, the self is performed,
which returns to my claim from the presentation
that there is no un-performed self.

And yet this irresistible urge toward honesty /
sincerity / getting it right, nakedness. A trust
that the performance is not "just" a performance,

that it communicates something of value. I can choose to be troubled my metaphysics or I can turn my attention toward ethical questions. Whether or not "I" "really" exists, I (often) feel like I do and in either case I face the same responsibility of figuring how to live. [I break from answering here to see if my cousin who is up reading Ramona is ready for some breakfast.]

[Returning the next morning:] But one problem you face is how your text will be received. Of course, you can't control the response and part of the magic is being open to the variety of readings that will follow, readings that are sometimes beyond the author.

Additionally, when you go to communicate, if you concentrate too much on the words you see that few of them hold water. Every word requires its own commentary because every word contains worlds. If* I† were‡ to§ try¶ to** explain†† I‡‡ would§§ first¶¶ have*** to††† explain‡‡‡ the§§§ whole¶¶¶ private**** history†††† of‡‡‡‡ asso-

---

* If
† I
‡ were
§ to
¶ try
** to
†† explain
‡‡ I
§§ would
¶¶ first
*** have
††† to
‡‡‡ explain
§§§ the
¶¶¶ whole
**** private
†††† history
‡‡‡‡ of

ciations[*] I[†] bring[‡] to[§] a[¶] word.[**] A private language is impossible, but each person's relationship with language is unique. *Genealogy* just doesn't do for you exactly what it does for me.

What, if any, are the essential differences between men and women (besides the obvious ones)?

Someone told me this story once about a writer who claimed that because he was a man he could not comment on the believability of female narrators. I think this is bullshit.

What's your technique for plate (painting) ten?

I took a magazine--I want to say a *Vanity Fair*, but I'm sure it was not that--and a blue pen that was running low on ink and traced along the spine repeatedly at what I eyeballed the proper distance. When I started, I had something different in mind--something much more uniform and colorful. The word that occurs to me now is *corporate*, which is possibly a way to reassure myself about abandoning the original idea. Scratch that. This is better: No. 10 is an object lesson in letting the project participate in / influence / determine its own outcomes. Project --> Product.

What's your absolute favorite book of poetry?

While working on <u>in vivo</u> it was *Howl and Other Poems*, especially "America."

Is writing a) a way of expanding the present? b)

---

[*] associations
[†] I
[‡] bring
[§] to
[¶] a
[**] word

a way of tracking the present? c) a way of repre-
senting the present? d) a way to create the pres-
ent?

Absolutely.

Just FYI, I read "beta blocker" as "betty crock-
er." This is not a question.

Is it a prescription, though?

Why do you go by The Synthesis instead of The An-
tithesis?

Sorry?

Antithesis, anti-thesis. This is your anti-thesis.

Anti-thesis by The Synthesis. Funny I never saw
that. Well, I've always been The Synthesis. So
that's nonnegotiable. And all this is always behind me anyway. I wrote the thesis, I wrote the
anti-thesis, and I just kept on writing--those two
projects will be mere footnotes in a vast library
of text.
    If I were going to take a negation seriously,
though, it wouldn't be a writing against but a
disintegration of some kind, a taking apart from
within. After the death of the author (the death
of the authorial persona) would follow the death
or dissolution of the text itself. I don't know
exactly what that would look like, but I think
it's the only way. You can read a text with no
author. How do you read a text with no text? Why
would you want to? Short of that, there's no undo-
ing The Synthesis. Even The Synthesis cannot undo
The Synthesis. Only nothingness, absolute nothingness. Form requires emptiness, emptiness requires
form. This would be something outside all that,
something completely meaningless, something I can-

not name, something that is not a something.

So, what does The Synthesis synthesize next?

CHAPTER 24: IN PASSING
[Eternity]

As I started to read over this manuscript for the first time to see what I needed to correct or redact* before I turned it into Monkey Puzzle to see if they were interested in publishing it, I asked myself whether the text accomplishes what it sets out to do. Has a memoir been written? Has something been gained?

Throughout the process it was oftentimes difficult to know what to write about without feeling lost. Structurally, it's obvious that I started out writing according to a calendar and shifted into writing about topics, maintaining the chronology insofar as the topics impressed themselves upon me more or less sequentially. It is no coincidence that time starts to break down in the text at the point I was undergoing a nearly constant wave of migraine and having my temporal sense somewhat scrambled in the process. As they cleared up in the spring, I was busy and stressed. I had to keep up with my teaching, my coursework, finishing my thesis, and looking for a job--all of which seemed like silly business in light of my uncle's passing. Living thusly day to day, event to event, assignment to assignment, travelling twice back to Portland to be with family, returning to find the program in disarray, I never found my way back to a regular schedule either for structuring experience or for recording it. These thematic episodes were written in short bursts as time allowed.

_____

* Correct as in fix mistakes, not as in revise or edit the material. Redact as in spare anyone who can be spared.

As the structure (d)evolved, I encouraged myself to trust in the project, trust that the subject would reveal itself through the writing. It was difficult, though, out on the front edge of everything. Every word I typed, as it is entered into the white space ahead and below, was a leap of faith into the unknown. It was of course like life in this respect (as was its goal), but we are rarely attuned in life to our faith in the future until a disaster is imminent. And writing a directionless book--even one as short as this--felt like the verge of disaster. Tracing the present into the future can't but draw one's attention to the fact that just as originality bears traces, traces spawn originality. When you start to fall there is no choice but to prepare for impact. I note my fear of heights and I continue.

If I am confirmed in my faith in the project it is by the soundness of its opening premise that as change is inevitable so too is the opportunity for memoir. Though the formal plans for in vivo were compromised by the content they shaped--or did not shape, as it turned out. This in a way is itself a lesson of memoir: the younger self who makes things like plans is constrained in time and denied access to things like outcomes or deviations. If I figure this out now (at least as it pertains to the timeline of in vivo) the project succeeds in performing this coming into knowing. The success, in other words, follows only from the failure. I know of no becoming that is not a death. Whatsoever will be an idea but a history we aren't yet able to write?

Before closing this account, I must address at least one stranger who haunts the text: Scott F. Parker. It is from the events of his days that I draw my story. I thank him for hosting this parasite and I return now his material so that he may draw upon it for his own ends. If I have made, for example, the thesis presentation sound like a bigger deal than it was, it was because the logic of the text (I felt) required it. To say the things we want to say, sometimes we must simply say them. If I have exposed some of his secrets, he will please take some comfort in knowing my intentions were pure.

God died for humanity the moment humanity understood they'd birthed god. So too The Synthesis.

Scott F. Parker writes: the above was composed (it is believed) in an underground library in Minneapolis. After writing it, The Synthesis was seen coming above ground into a sunny summer afternoon. The observer blinked and The Synthesis vanished. He has not been seen since.

It is my sincerest understanding that as every I gives way to some other I, and as every being exists only insofar as it participates in becoming, The Synthesis had to die to become what will follow him--he disappeared himself so as to be replaced by what will eventually grow of his remnants. As the chain of causation is without beginning or end, The Synthesis's first utterance was to ask, "How can I begin with this," to which he knew the answer that there is no preparation for beginning any more than there is a beginning to a beginning. The end of The Synthesis is similarly mysterious. Because the observer blinked, we do not know where The Synthesis ended or where he ends or what it could mean for him to end when all end is transition.

What we knew as The Synthesis appears to be gone, but this is more a comment on what we knew than on the nature of The Synthesis.

The nature of The Synthesis . . . I will do as it seemed he wanted and send off his manuscript. After that, I will leave The Synthesis, as he has left me.

IN PEACE

*Nor is it a relation of synthesis between the One (the Real) and language.
It is a non-relation, a "unilateral duality."*
—Laruelle

CONTENTS*

*Among the Synthesis's papers, the following pages were discovered. These texts have been selected from a larger cache and arranged for publication but are otherwise unedited. —ed.

IF AS IF

If it's written right it will read as if it lives as it was composed entirely in a brick-walled cafe where I—a thousand I's—lie tucked away in a corner with a view of the sidewalk and half a cup of lukewarm coffee. A whiskey hangover, worn books in front of me, ink on my fingers, today a cigarette break from yesterday.

(IN SERIES)

in there
in time
in order
in contrast
in()action
in solidarity
in haste
in due time
in no time
in your head
in words
inwards
in a sack of skin
in the event of my demise
in any case
in fact
inevitably
inbent
in progress
in(finite) series

THE BOOK

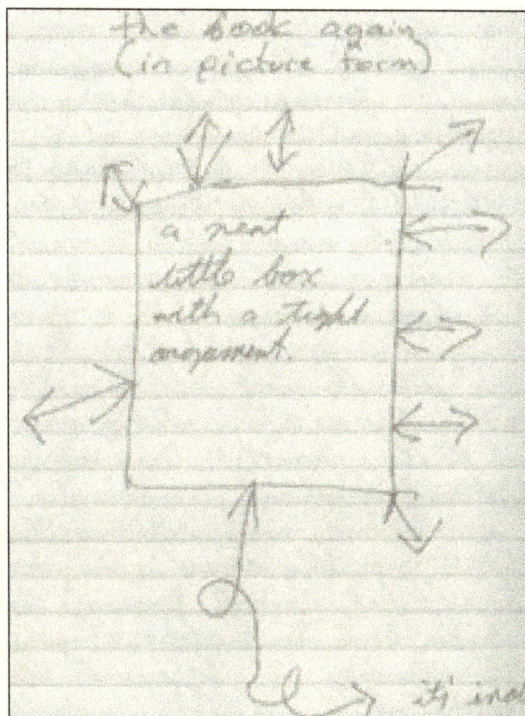

JANUARY 30

The radio is silenced as I plumb away. This coffee has cooled, but its presence at my hand is reassuring. The brown ring staining the mug is a wobbly disk of history. A white porcelain story that probably started in China. I run my fingernails up my neck in a backhanded motion and the sound is as textured as the touch. The outside world is slippery today with ice. The shine is translucent despite the drabness of the sky and the steam wafting from the building across the alley. The cat stretches, returns to sleeping. The simple everything we witness while we wait.

BENEATH

beneath what makes us who we *are* lies what *makes us* who we are:

the morning constitutional
the emotional comfort gained from time spent wandering the aisles of chain
bookstores
the tendency to over-caffeinate
the large stretches of day still devoted to sexual fantasies
the lack of patience when the world declines to conform to desires
the day after day failure to live up to aspirations
the relief that comes with another day of rain
the times you surprise yourself

the tone of voice you take with your wife and the tone she takes with you when
   once again the dishes are undone, the refrigerator empty, and you're late for
   work
   (do you find grace in that moment? do you look for it?)

the people you give yourself to on a daily basis
   (yesterday was forever)

beneath the ideals are the human truths that this tastes better than that and sometimes our tastes are all that we taste
the music you listen to
the TV shows you don't watch
the books you read
the books you write
the persona(e) you present to the world(s) vs. the person you feel like to yourself
   and
the constant movement in the space between (between the multitude)

instructive is the amount of resentment you hang onto when you are imposed
   upon
—are you the giant off whose back water drips heated by the fire of your appetite

—are you Atlas?
—are your knees weak this day?
—do you feel the mosquitoes of life or do you walk unbitten by parasites?
—and can you choose? can you choose?

all the things you can't point at but never doubt for a second
the things you feel in the air
the song that appears in your head when you're happy
the strange habit of smelling your toenail clippings
memories of the times you were lucky and the promises you've made
the secret prayer for a cancellation
the fear you would never admit to
the fear of admitting to fear
juxtaposed to the desire to reassure
the need to save everyone
the stubborn refusal to be saved
the bone need for the outdoors
the contentment to sit with words and the dead
the constant sense of failure
the reassurance that the sense of failure leads to achievement
the knowledge that achievement doesn't lead to happiness
the foolishness of hoping for new results from the same methods
the stubbornness
the stubbornness
the blessing and the curse of an active mind
the lives unlived
the jealousy
the pettiness
the judgment
the fear
the ego
the knowledge that everything I've thought of *I've* thought of
the pride
the parasitic pride
the loneliness
the unreasonable frequency with which email is checked

the recognition when Mary Karr says her head thought it could kill her and keep
    on living
when a student says we must act rather than think our way out of problems
when an uncle defines *implosion*
when you work so hard only to become what you always were

220

the frustration with fragmentation
the pervasiveness, the absoluteness, of fragmentation
the need for absolution
the disbelief in absolution
the tiredness
the tiredness

the fantasies
the weaknesses (not) given into
the disappointments
the judgments
the strong moral voice that comes from nowhere but everywhere
the learning in every moment anew how to live
and sometimes failing
sometimes failing
sometimes failing
sometimes failing
sometimes failing
sometimes failing
sometimes failing
sometimes failing
choosing eventually
to let failure
go

OF ALONENESS

Sometimes people will tell me I like to be alone as much as I do because I'm introverted, as if that explains anything. Yes, I want to tell them, and it's sunny today because there aren't any clouds. I wish there were clouds. Then it's less likely I'd be be made a tautology.

I prefer to be alone, though even admitting so feels like a failure. They don't make movies about recluses anymore—or if they do they condense a life into one romantic montage. I don't want to be montaged anymore than I want to be defined out of existence. I'd rather define myself into existence in real time.

NOTES ON THE UR-TEXT

The written word spoken, the spoken word recorded, the recorded word archived, the archives opened: the themes of the ur-text resounding.

See: a man—in an image, *me*—sprawled out on the couch, boxers and a blazer: coffee, Adderall canister with the prescription rubbed off, dime bag, more coffee, and more.

He is wearing himself out to wake himself up. This is only a short nap, a brief respite amidst perpetual struggle. He is too young to know the meaning of perpetual. The struggle is interminable, but every moment is endurable. And when he looks back he won't see himself as having endured but as having triumphed. Only he knows where he started, only he knows where he will never arrive. If he's singing to himself, it's the song where Dylan says he not busy being born is busy dying.

Hi. Allow me to reintroduce myself. My name is . . .

The Synthesis was here.

LOOKING OUT

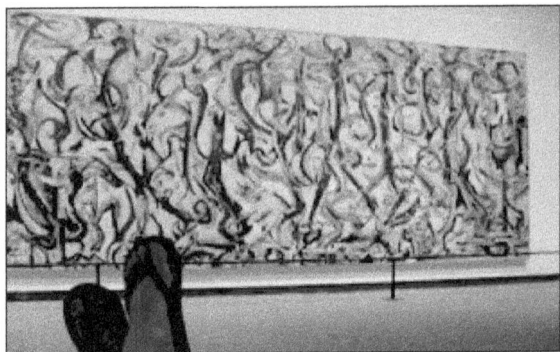

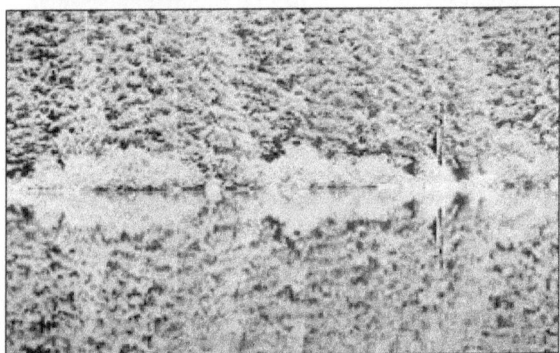

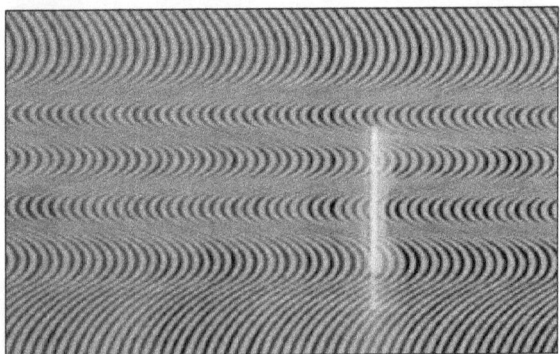

LOST AND FOUND SELF IN TIME

Already one to mourn the slippage of time, beginning at age twelve I used to take a lot of pictures. I'd be inclined to say "around age twelve," but I'm staring at the evidence: here's Haystack Rock, occluded by fog on the Oregon coast; here's a water fountain from Portland's Japanese Garden; and here are my friends at a baseball game—all shot on an old 110mm camera that has left flat-colored and ancient-seeming prints. (A year later I enjoyed the switch to a better 35mm camera and the pictures show it.) It felt imperative to the younger me—to so many of them, really—to leave a record—not so much for posterity as for my own future selves. I wanted one day to be able to remember who I'd been. And so I was compelled to constantly produce archiveable evidence of a life fully lived: adventures had, phases entered into and abandoned, friends made, not forgotten, experiences experienced. I planned to look back as an adult, just as I was already looking back as an adolescent, discerning wisdom from the six-year-old me that the fourteen-year-old me had lost access to and was determined to regain. This future remembering in sight, the camera was my weapon against time's passing, the force with which I could make it last.

Last as what but memory, though? The present collected as future past. The logical conclusions easily identified: that final moment before death when everything would finally be complete, when the story would finally reach a resolution. That and the all-out sprint to get there. Life flashing along with the camera before my eyes the first time around. Like all greedy people never happy, there I was lost in time.

But then the era of everyone with a camera 24/7, of Google Maps letting you see almost anything on Earth from your bedroom, of PhotoShop making it so that no one could assume any longer that an image represented something like the "real."

The ubiquity and fluidity of the photographic image has rendered it neither special nor reliable. It's clear that pictures don't preserve the past as much as they communicate certain fantasies of the past. PhotoShop makes gross the subtler editing work of the discarded print, the discerning photographic eye. The hundreds of pictures on your phone and your Facebook promise thousands more, few of them worth a comment let alone a thousand words.

Nevertheless, I fear I have fully absorbed the ideology of persona that saturates our culture: that a life must be lived in public to be said to exist in any substantial way; that being is a product of having been witnessed, reported, recorded, and distributed. The representations, as Baudrillard said, are more real than what they're representations of. *Esse est percipi*—and hopefully online somewhere you can get a lot of likes. Intellectually, of course, it's easy to reject this line of thought, but the ideology of the image—and the idolatry—is buried too deep within me to so far be excavated. It's not a way of seeing the world that I chose to adopt and it's not one I've so far succeeded in shaking.

David Shields calls Facebook personal essay for people who can't write. The site offers an explicit opportunity to produce the kind of public persona a person previously required celebrity to attain. You might think—as I might—that such a platform would be a natural fit for the Synthesis. However, something about the proliferation of sharing the transparently selective and manipulative versions of self* that are presented online leaves me feeling plastic—not malleable, though: cheap and disposable.

In her essay "Generation Why?" Zadie Smith calls out the reductivity of Facebook's features, the way it squeezes the self into discrete data considered important by a college student and later his corporate backers. But this is not a call to arms in defense of the real or a plea that we somehow return to it. Human relationships are always mediated and selves are always contingent (in part) upon the culture. As Smith points out, novels too are reductive, but the good ones a lot less so than the bad ones, not to mention self-promoting social networking websites. It's only in retrospect that Facebook appears significant in what I'm thinking of as a shifting relationship to time.

So why are we so concerned to update our Facebook pages in order to influence how we're seen by others? Why did I find it necessary to photograph so many events of my early life? I wanted, I think, as many of us want, to be at the center of a story people demanded to hear and, more, *to see*. So I told such a story, one where the supporting evidence—not even *what* was recorded but the very thoroughness of the recordings—proved the importance of the subject, proved it to some eventual audience—even if that audience would only be an older me. Evidence that I existed, that my life mattered, that it was worth preserving.

Such an attitude speaks of a devaluation of experience. When I look at my photos now, I see a life lived with an eye toward the camera, an ironic distancing adopted in the hope that the material would work better in retrospect than it did in the moment. The major problem with it is that evidence of having existed is not evidence of existence. The payoff can never reach you, even if you post your photos the minute you take them. You'll always be waiting to see the moment

---

* (But how do you win? Not being on Facebook, I'm performing and sharing a version of self—one who is aloof or indifferent or in some manner too good—just as much as if I were on it.)

from the other side. Your nostalgia becomes you.

Perhaps by now I've seen enough death to be less sentimental toward life. I find myself less inclined to want to preserve what can't be preserved. I no longer look at pictures as often as I once did, and in general I spend less time with my head turned over my shoulder. When I was a kid I used to think our experience of time's passing was directly related to the portion remaining. As the slippage accelerates, I worry less about making it last. I'm more inclined now to enjoy a day on the beach with my family, swimming in the ocean and playing bocce on the sand, without having to project myself into the future to see if I enjoyed myself—or to confirm that I was really there. It is more likely now that it is enough for me to participate without having also to witness.

Too: a first-person narration. It isn't a big leap to imagine that the written documentation has replaced the photographed for me. I don't "record" my experiences in writing the way I did with the camera, but I do still produce versions of what happened that stand for—and often replace—the events themselves. Whether it's the purpose or a byproduct of employing the "I" in this fashion the effect is the same: the "I" becomes a constructed self that can live in the perpetual present of the text (as long as the text survives). By storing versions of myself, partial though they are, outside my own memory I retain the chance in some strange way to live forever—at least those parts the prose captures.

When I took pictures they were an aid to memory so that I would always be able to access the past. When I write now it's to try to understand something that confounds me. The struggle against time, the struggle in time. The self made artifact, the artifact made eternal.

LOOKING IN

LOOKING AWAY

The true mysteries of existence can set loose such a torrent of doubt and confusion in our minds when we so little as name them (mortality, identity, evil, consciousness, existence itself) that for the sake of day-to-day comfort we'll go to great lengths to avoid thinking about them.

False certainty and blatant avoidance are our most effective and addictive methods. The former in the form of religion or other ideologies that allow us to put the problems off to the side, as if to say, Glad that's taken care of. The latter through distractions—be they drugs and alcohol, pornography and television, or consumerism and other self-indulgences—which we use to pretend there aren't problems in the first place.

But if we've gotten far enough to see that ignorance is bliss we've gone too far for ignorance to be a real possibility. A fact doesn't cease to be a fact when you don't look at it, and a problem doesn't cease to be a problem when you look away from it.

When we choose willful ignorance and blunted consciousness because it makes our lives easier in the short term we are left susceptible to surprise attacks from the mysteries of consciousness in the long term. In choosing to escape consciousness we do not escape the conscious choice to escape, and in this fundamental condition lies the existential truth: we cannot in good faith look away. If we try we'll find before too long, when we're least prepared and most vulnerable, these mysteries come back for us. In "The Crack-Up," Fitzgerald wrote, "in a real dark night of the soul, it is always three o'clock in the morning."

He wrote in the same essay, echoing Keats's negative capability, that "the test of a first-rate intelligence is the ability to hold two opposed ideas in the mind at the same time, and still retain the ability to function." To be human means (at its best) being willing to take a long look at the mysteries and try not to be, but ultimately accept that you are, somewhat confused. And what do we gain by these efforts? I wish I could promise happiness, but we wouldn't go through our elaborate self-deceptions if it was happiness we were avoiding. Some lucky few will, as a consequence of their genuine interrogations, find satisfying responses to the mysteries of existence, and maybe even happiness. With envy, more of us will not. But in risking looking into the dark mysteries we'll have, if nothing else, some honesty. Is that enough? It better be, because what choice do we have?

(Something like that is how I put myself to sleep at night.)

AT THE MOMENT

i'm studying a poem
i mean a painting
if it is a painting
it's a photograph i'm looking at
in my study
things are not what they seem
i remember the echo
every infinitesimal makes an impression
on the locus of my contentment
outside there's snow on the river
take a seat
in a museum time slows down
in a hollowed-out season it about stops
the bench too is a work of art
these are dangerous spaces
i don't mind abstractions
it is the spirit that falls into the void
this room was empty before i arrived
& it's empty now
hexagon hexagon, diamond diamond, rectangle rectangle
square
poetry licks the wounds
i like this painting
if it is a painting &
i am not in pain
nor am i here to communicate
i'm here to breathe
this year like last year
like tomorrow
a lucky break
forms in this anxious place

THE SYNTHESIS BY THE SYNTHESIS

S: What would you like to be asked?

S: I would like to be asked what it is like.

S: Say.

S: It is like this. It is this. This is it.

S: That's it?

S: That's it.

S: Is it not also some other way? Ever?

S: You're thinking of emptiness.

S: I am.

S: And what if you do not? What if you are not?

S: But we must communicate. We must participate.

S: Indeed.

S: And in deed.

S: We become compassion.

S: How so?

S: Through practice. A story: There was a boy who slept with a stuffed rabbit. The rabbit comforted the boy and allowed him to not see demons at night. When he learned of an earthquake in a far off land and heard that children there were in need, he packed up his rabbit and asked his mom to send it off. His mom asked if he wouldn't rather give some of the stuffed animals in his closet, the ones he never used. He said, it wouldn't mean anything if I give them those ones.

S: Is that true?

S: You mean, did it happen? To me? I can't remember.

S: Is compassion so cryptic?

S: You're right. Ask me another question.

S: What are your origins?

S: I was born here and I'll die here. My will is irrelevant. Before introducing the Synthesis, I was conceived somewhere between the smoky last calls in Eugene, Oregon, and the morning stumble for coffee, a notepad, and some days a cheap breakfast. It was a place where jazz and spoken word bounced around the speakerbox and you could walk outside and find friends in any alleyway, and these friends knew way more about everything than you did. I say you, but I mean *I*. I was young—I was unborn!—but I was curious. That curiosity is my god. It was a time—maybe the last time—when time still rambled and took occasional detours, a time when you could get everything done and still watch the sun go behind the mountain, a time when mushrooms grew on trees, when trees were bountiful, and the bounty was ours.

> I'm first from an idea, my moment helpless telos participant.
> I'm the product of evolution and theory,
> > so many possibilities bumping heads.
> I'm from the edge of the vast still sea,
> > from under the Doug-firs, moss like insulation for time.
> I'm from barefoot summer streets
> > and sweaty night times of optimism.
> I'm from where my sister's from,
> > from where my cousins are from,
> > from where the pink sky appears
> > as if an improbable promise.
> I'm from rain on rooftops and enchanted forests
> > comforting the discomforted.
> I'm from wherever that water touches down,
> > regardless of whether thoughts make noise.

S: What do you hope to accomplish?

S: I hope to write honestly and without fear.

S: How will you know if you've succeeded?

S: In a way, I'm not sure that's for me to answer. I will have succeeded if readers—if *one* reader—picks up my work and feels like it's bringing them more fully to life, making them more fully conscious of existence, her life more full of meaning. I see it as a matter of texture. Reality is dense with meaning but that meaning is only concomitant to our capacity for wonder. I want to draw attention to the texture, to provoke wondering. And in so doing I'm always up against the limits of my own wonder, my own imagination, my own creativity. One hopes, working at his highest capacity, to somehow break new ground, knowing all the while that if he succeeds that ground will be incomprehensible (until his eyes adjust) or uninhabitable—or he will have become unrecognizable to himself. It's a chance. There's no promise of reward. And it's a high bar, but I never understood why in a life that ends you'd try for anything less. I want to write like life is at stake because I think it is.

S: Who or what is your antithesis?

S: The Synthesis is big. The Synthesis contains all. But all of what? One part thesis, one part antithesis, as the gloss on Hegel has it. But each synthesis faces its own antithesis as the spiral expands. The Synthesis is not a thing, not really a person, but a process. So my antithesis? Only what's waiting for me. I hope to find out.

S: How should your work be read?

S: I don't want to be too prescriptive. It's like all reading, each makes the text her own. However, this project is not one that will reach conclusion. I'm not sure what it would mean to conclude it. At some point, by one cause or another, I will simply break off writing. I don't see how it could be read expect in this light. In that sense, it remains open, the reader is let in but must find her own escape. Not simply putting the book down, but leaving the text behind, regardless of whether it turns out I wrote the text or you did. What's it like in here? You tell me. I mean it. You tell me.

S: Do you take this very seriously?

S: Yes and no. Yes in that it matters to me. No in the sense of being some kind of burden. It is rather a joy. But I am aware that others do not always see it this way.

S: What a pity.

S: For you or for them?

S: What difference does it make?

S: Then tell them.

S: I fear it will make no difference. I write what I would like to read. What else is there to say?

S: Can you say why?

S: Consciousness struggling with itself, seeking to tell a story that is self-accounting and complete in its necessary incompleteness, a form that is pliable enough to include the reader, material that shapeshifts at the touch, so many books are this way, so much art, the rivers and the trees, the breath of life, the inhale, the exhale, the pause between—

S: I love that pause!

S: That's the idea. To write a book, a line, these notebook scraps, whatever, that lives entirely in that pause. The matrix in which action occurs. That action itself, who cares?

S: Something of an idealist then.

S: So it seems! But no, I don't think so, not really. It is a fine thing that I'm sitting in *this* cafe, drinking *this* cup of coffee, listening to this music coming out of the speakers—a fine thing! It is even a fine thing to share the details of this moment. However, the sharing interests me more than what is shared. If the music is Elliott Smith or the Shins does not matter except insofar as it matters to the text, the filter. That filter is always limited—and therefore never ideal—specific. It becomes broader only as it comes to stand for, to represent, other cases.

You don't find yourself in other texts, what you find is yourself represented by another. In a word, communion. Pessoa said, "I am, in large measure, the selfsame prose I write." Whether the self is constructed or deconstructed, it becomes largely a linguistic matter. Everything is inner to the I. The dream is on equal ground with waking life. But that solipsism is challenged for the reader by a book that shares its subjectivity. I think it's about learning how to love and be loved, the various kinds of acceptance that requires.

S: What is it like existing only in a text?

S: Is it only in a text that I exist? How can I answer this?

S: Try.

S: That's what I'm trying to do. In his memoir, Barthes says, "It must all be considered as if spoken by a character in a novel."

S: And?

S: We must think, but thinking is not enough. Being is a being.

S: Even for a thought?

S: Even for a thought. Especially for a thought.

THE CONDITION

Just as I would turn off my reading lamp and let myself release the strain of being seven years old, it would start. Darting about my bedroom, escaping to that corner as I pursued it to this one, evading my direct attention but remaining on the periphery of my consciousness, this energy, silent but raging; I knew it was in my head—the voices you cannot quiet usually are—but I was helpless to contain it. Alone in the dark with only this torment, I waited. Waited until I recognized in the energy my condition and, at last, could sleep.

TRUTH & HAPPINESS

The struggle between truth and happiness could leave a certain kind of person scratching at his head as if trying to rip up the ground where the battle is taking place. Taken to its conclusion this strategy is effective, but short of suicide the approach can't but re-entrench the respective sides and redouble truth's stronghold because of course for anyone who picks such a fight the victor is already chosen. In any fight that happiness would win there is no fight to begin with.

But truth always advances on a battlefield. Whether against previous or competing truths/truth claims or against the comatose seduction of oblivion. We must turn our minds off if we're to function, and yet how can we in a world that needs our attention. N. found grace in oblivion. N. also knew how serious it was that god is dead. Truth and happiness decoupled—and a choice that is not a choice. Or maybe there is a choice. A choice to choose when to go for truth and when to get let go of it.

METAPHYSICAL NOTE TO SELF

Sitting here failing alone to live,
Purging the absolute vacuity of my consciousness—
Little nothings floating
Briefly from nowhere
Bound for annihilation—
Faithful that with patience
The insight will burst through
Like a fish from a lake
That I am a kind with them
And we'll cease to cling to cling to cling.

ON WRITING

It's still dark when I wake up,
Even in June, it's still dark when I wake up.
I open my laptop. There isn't a moment to lose.
I open my laptop and find the white screen where the worlds will go.
And, slowly, I begin filling in the words:
I write *the* and I write *time* and I write *memory*
And it's important to be concrete
so when I remember I put in a noun like *potato*
or *Cincinnati,*
an adjective like *prickly*—no, *pugnacious.*
More than any other word I write *I.*
I'm not writing about myself, it's just that I is a common word in English.
I'm not writing about myself now either.
I'm not writing about writing either.

Despite what the title says, this isn't writing—
this is the mania by which I don't kill myself.

Do not underestimate the seriousness of *have to*
to someone who's been up all night
in a dark room with the lights out on purpose.

I keep the brain buzz burning as long as there's coffee in my cup
I can't think on nothing
I'm trying to learn about the history of economic alienation and brush up
on the latest trends in French philosophy
but my feet are too warm in boots
and the lady at the counter
has things she wishes to communicate too.

I wait.
I am patient.
I am waiting.

The braided snakes on the back of the head in front of me don't belong to Medu-
sa
and I am curious about the state of French philosophy business, very curious,
but the thing is I'm made of electricity and brains
are not muscles.

See I learned something about survival:
when people say "people" they don't mean
people, they mean something smaller.
Writing won't save my life.
Writing is a parasite
and I'm alive because I have so much blood in me.
Lives aren't saved (*from what?*)
They're nourished   or they are not.

I encourage people because I want so badly to be encouraged.

We are so simple.
I say "nourish me" and
I am nourished.

And it goes on: humming along
the pop of the keypad when you really get a rhythm going tap tap tap tap
burn off the energy before it pools up and explodes.
Life is the fuel for the light and
the light passing through the windowshade is not light at all.

What I found is I write to make sense of the world,
to put order to chaos,
I write to say to the world all the things I need the world to say to me.
I'm trying to love my way out of fear
(Maybe this is about me.)

I used to take Adderall at midnight and write until sunrise without blinking,
when I would climb a ladder up to the roof and watch Portland turn pink
or stay gray,
the nighttime hours already burned,
the lingering traces that seeped out the windows
now evaporating in sunlight.
Some of us would stay here forever.

POEM OF THE INTEROBJECTIVE ME

Impossible to say who I is.

Or how real I'm made.

Rhyme to get laid, blow up like the [censored for radio]

You should not use the word poem when talking about me, but I think in interobjective you must

use the word *objective.*

I'm twenty-three years old. I might just be my mother's child, but in all reality, I'm everybody's child.

Society raised me.

Society, menace to.

I feel sorry for your mother.

But also, he adds, Reality is wrong. Dreams are for real. A direct quote.

*

I used to read *Enlightenment* magazine.

Buddha and dharma up in that glossy sheen.

This me knows because the sangha says it's so.

And me takes refuge in the we-facts, so relax:

me + nature > me + poetry

∴ (by additive property of order*) nature > poetry

(or all poetry is nature poetry)

(or or culture is a subset of bread//the better part of wine is water→)

And how we are thirsty!

We are starving ourselves to live.

I am writing poetry from the anorectic!

I am writing notes to all anorectics! (There's nothing casual about this.)

As me approaches zero, the equation still holds.

But me is not greater than zero.

Equality is tautology in the land of the shrinking members.

Me is not always greater than zero.

        *

My seven-year theory is a creation story:

Puzzle pieces misarranged on the fold-out card table

for perpetuity as my grandma's wig slides from her head.

"White meat or dark?" someone asks at dinner, "Take a piece."

It all tastes the same in here: dry and chewey like when the clock stuck.

There's more meat.

I cut the pork chop in little pieces and slide them

one by one

off the table, into my fist, which I move gently to my lap

---

* Assuming me ≥ 0.

241

and then into my pocket. This takes time.

But when I'm done I have a pocket full of pork to throw into the neighbors'
yard, where the

raccoons will find it tonight.

It's clear to me I've grown in so many ways.

*

There are other we-facts, some of them true:

Some of them documented.

Notebooks, photographs, etc. Memories.

Some survive, some were burned in the fire of self-creation.

Which is a literal fire,

objectively point-out-able via the ash still under my nails.

I walked through it.

Everybody knows that. Everybody.

Ask them.

Ask them.

Ask.*

---

* Many of the lines are either adaptations from Ronaldo Wilson's *Poems of the Black Object* or
from Biggie Smalls's "Juicy," which Wilson refers to repeatedly in an interview about his book.
Modeling the influence Biggie had on Wilson, I incorporated lines from Tupac and other cultural
landmarks from my 1990s. Other lines were sparked by associations or misreadings of other lines
of Wilson's, with the remainder generated from what I saw as the poem's emerging logic. And that
logic, if I had to name it, would center around the piecemeal construction of the self through the ac-
cumulation of some of those discrete "facts" that have survived in memory (truly, or with the boost/
alteration of some form of documentation: social or artificial). It's a poem that, if I wanted it to be,
could be almost endless. There's effectively no limit to the number of stories or influences I could
include. I tried to keep the sources somewhat restrained for now to stick sort of tightly to the jumping off points listed above, but thematically there's no reason it couldn't keep expanding outward.

THE SICKNESS

I am in a cafe. The coffee is good, the pastries are bad. Outside, a stray dog scrounges for something to eat. I'd give him my croissant, but really I am in the suburbs and there is no stray dog. In truth, I am on the internet, there is nothing outside. The sickness in me is spiritual. The case, I fear, is terminal. I have never been hypochondriacal. I have always been prone to psychosomatic suffering. Which begs the question, the *always* does.

If there were a dog outside, it would be looking for water not food—and some shade to rest in. It will be a long afternoon. Like the dog, my nausea has become nauxious. It spirals of itself. It loops, it perpetuates, it will demolish. It is a matter of time.

How will I maintain if, indeed, I will maintain? Will I finish my work before the sickness ~~envelopes~~ extinguishes me?

Patterns emerge long after they have transpired, in retrospect. I see now that I have committed grievous harm to myself over the years. A knife cannot cut itself, lips cannot kiss themselves. The human being is not a knife, not a pair of lips. I have always been better with a knife.

Someone close to me accepted a ride from an intoxicated driver. My interjections failed to dissuade her. Unable to bear the possibilities, I took a bottle cap and gouged two divots in my forearm. The pain soothed me until I could confirm her safety.

It is imperative to some core part of me that I suffer most.

Self-righteousness.

Self-fulfilling prophecy.

Positive feedback loop.

I get what I want.

This is the nature of the condition.

But there is erasure without violence.

I work not so that I might live but that for a little while longer I might not die. The mania by which I don't kill myself? Writing empties me out, not like sex or a marathon. Like blunt trauma. It takes and takes long past the time when I have something left to spare. This might be a lesson, or it might be a punishment. There are many ways to not exist.

If my works survive me, they will have killed me. If I survive them, it will mean I survived myself and survived my life until its end.

I hate the idea of sacrificing for art. Let art sacrifice for me. I want to be the kind of artist who leaves no traces. The kind who it's possible was not there.

A true work of art? Transcending the need to exist.

To take another tack: to not compound suffering with suffering; to let the writing write itself; to effortlessly make no effort; to do nothing and leave nothing undone; to hug with no arms; to allow the nausea to absolve itself; to accept; to swim; to participate; to love; to live; to die; to not mind the difference.

SLEEP AS METAPHYSICS

What do I think about as I fall asleep?
Wittgenstein says, "Whereof we cannot speak, thereof we must remain silent."
What do I think about as I fall asleep?
Everything depends on how we choose to understand *must*.
I pursue silence.
Thoughts link with thoughts to form a chain leading into the void, enfolding.
The trick is to get to where you can't tell if you're inventing the future or
    unfolding it.
I lie suspended, a bridge between existence and non-.
We have no recourse to truth, only to utility, and N. says,
"No small art is it to sleep: it is necessary for that purpose to keep awake all
    day."
If this is an art, I want to craft paradox—
and breathe presence in absence,
maintain awareness of the exact moment when
form and emptiness dissolve.
Call thinking binary or dissolution ultimately synthetic,
an emptiness beyond the emptiness that makes form possible,
I still want to sleep with eyes open and witness my own annihilation.
The period when you can't tell if you're awake or asleep is the best time to ask
    yourself: Why is there something rather than nothing?
And what is the ontological nature of time?
The circle circles itself.
And a question asked in words cannot be answered in anything else.
These logics are nontransferable.
Meanwhile, pushing the line a little farther back with each word-anchor, I build
    things.
I build territories. I put shelter in these territories and take refuge there.
You take refuge where you find it.
Maybe in N., the word, and the self.
Whereof we believe not, we extinguish not.
And refuges are fires from which we've started to gather light and heat we can-
    not hold.

So I sleep with the window open. There's vigor in wilful futility.
I'm skillful in the means of contra-
diction within the fiction of my chosen -ism:
These memories occur in language.
This language occurs in context. This context is given. This given is got.
And so my dreams are contingent dreams.
Yet I interpret them absolutely:
storms obliterating everything in their paths
all lights extinguished
and no one left to dream of nothing.
Eventually, awaiting my storm, world becomes word
and
whereof I remain silent, thereof

FRAGMENTS

I might as well be a writer. My whole life is narrated in my head as it happens anyway, jumping between other's perspectives and perspectives I'll hold in the future.

I've known this for years, why write it down now?

If you don't ever decide, you decide by default.

I'm pulled in every direction. Will one direction win out or will the vectors continue to cancel?

Asking the question has become the practice.

The simple philosophy of Marcus Aurelius is a comfort and crutch for getting through the day.

Still sitting but not sitting still.

So many voices many voices I can't tell which is . . . they're all inside me . . . the filter is faulty.

Note to a future lover: I find myself on every page. Maybe you're in here too.

My wisdom: love is the key more than wisdom, and the word *love* means love, urgent and overwhelming.

Certainty: to talk about something there must be something, and we must know there is something. We know there is something. Do we know there is knowing? We must know there is knowing before we can know there is something. Knowing knowing precedes knowing something. The knowing that knowing knowing precedes knowing something precedes knowing knowing. But I don't know if I know only some of these things.

I like my art sad and my life happy—but if you don't keep enough melancholy around you risk forgetting art.

. . . something happens and I'm reminded that I am an object in the world, as well as a subject—and once again there is I and I is alone, self-conscious, afraid.

So often the mind slips into old habits, rethinking thoughts it's thought a thousand times. Remember the time . . . ? Yes, I remember And I remembered. And I'll go on remembering. And if I don't?

No light without dark, no life without death, no Synthesis without not-Synthesis.

It's always 3 a.m. in my notebook.

If that clock on the wall stops ticking we could stay here forever, in this dark place where only we exist.

Trapped in my bodymind.

I'm not even a writer, I just play one in real life.

Life is an explosion from context//Not everything is translatable into language.

That was going to be the point. But then I went to lunch.

What to do after doneness? Another project is needed: work on the Synthesis ( ).

Everyone is proven wrong by time, especially those who are proven right.

If we begin with our ends in mind we shortchange our beginnings, for they exist only as the means of reaching the end. Why not, then, just get to the point and start with the end? Discovery can be an end iff it is sumultaneously not an end. The love of wisdom is self-contained. Any outside appeal is either unsatisfactory or contradictory.

The argument I'm developing about the relationship between politics and consciousness depends entirely on the time I got jumped when I was eleven years old, not to mention a thousand other accidents.

1) There is no absolute autonomy. Think of the most autonomous situation. Now think of the first one hundred things that autonomy is dependent on or limited by.

2) There are no absolute statements, including 1) and 2). Ditto: direct causality exists in logic but never in the so-called real world. Ditto: on any one level, autonomy is equal for all, so while there is no absolute autonomy, relative autonomy is equal, so while no one is in complete control of one's life . . . more generally: I'll let it take any form it asks for. There are no rules when there are no rules.

Synthesis was a great noticer . . . but not much happened to the Synthesis. One thing he noticed was that while he was busy noticing what was happening, he could have been out happening.

Synthesizing as a way of life.

The meaning I take from any moment past occurs now. Writing about an epiphany, I must create a new one.

—try to language my way out of language until time runs out on all these limitations.

An artist: someone who *makes* things and *gives* them to people.
An artist: someone who has perfected self-consumption.

Reading note: the story you think you're reading is not the story you are actually reading. It moves sideways on you and you are where?

No one is more generative than N. After he tore everything down, we can't help but see where to start building back up. He reads like a good earthworm, chewing through our waste to make our soil rich, from which we blossom.

N. was right when he said he was the future. The question now is who will be the future. Religion is still possible, we just need better gods.

This + this + that + maybe some of those.

It's a relief to find you were right to trust—I say trust—that things are connected & what's connected to you is to sit in real time where/when you stop thinking about & then stop seeing & eventually start writing the connection in words running all the way down from this parchment page to the old familiar pain bellowing in my back right knee need to run by summer lake & treetop glow at rhythm where feet cease touching ground & no one checks their email or even has any email to check—that, David Shields, is how literature saved my life.

If sanity means having a story of self that is compatible with "reality," in a changing world the only universal story of self is the story of selflessness—the ur-self the un-self—& telling this story to oneself is the way.

in here comes out soon. Writing about self interests me as literature/art, but I'm dreading the consequences of that, that this "self" is going to have to deal w/ "out here."

The mad ramblings in a young man's notebook whether or not the man is actually very young, or indeed a man.

& but what is this but a fear of nonexistence that I wasn't aware belong to me (that I wasn't aware I belonged to)?

Syntax dreams: don't hesitate to speak in them.

ocean impressions
van Gogh reminds that
style is everything
everything is style
style communicates
style is communicated
style is the message
style is influence
experiments come through
           come out of
style is law
what matters is how
the what is in the how
expression as message
vision translatable

The yogi says you have to want it more than you fear it, want it more than you fear it.

Nothing is more American than America, said Bob Dylan, who is a genius.

If I had a reason to write this, I wouldn't.

no margins, only the thing itself—we are the mirror—

~~Why I am a destiny!~~ Why I am a possibility!

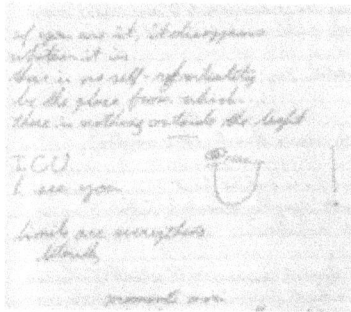

Notes on nervous illness: I've never known a person with schizophrenia not to be working on a proof of . . . everything . . . and I've never known myself to not think that's very impressive.

It's lovely here when it's lovely here.

My Struggle
"It becomes art, but never more than that."
Is there more than that?

What makes literature special as art form is access to inner life—in a world that can do everything else, what about a literature that does only that?

Ongoing search for time: rereading of course a way to encounter what can't be re-encountered.

Letting your mind speak someone else's voice, be careful whose.

The voices never stop talking, but you learn how to stop listening to them.

Ars essaica: I don't remember my earliest memories and I'm not sure I ever did.

SAMSARA

The question is how you see yourself in these scenes, people, and landscapes. You are there, in the masks and the molten lava, and in the songs of the human voice erupting from the cosmos as from the body. So much suffering perpetuated but so much magic too—attend to negation or attend to affirmation? What we have is like a duty. We do our part neither with resignation nor with expectation. And there's parts of us that remember everything if we access those parts—it goes all the way back. Each of us has a unique relationship with our history. Mine plays these themes in this time and yours speaks a language I can't hear, let alone understand—and nothing is closer to us than our language. It's not private, it's personal. Personal joy, personal need, and personal crazy. All really here even as it will be washed away.

LIBRARY BUILDING

As our information needs evolve so too does our arrangement of our information. Unsearchable technologies bound by memory as much as by glue or thread. Margit Ahmann's cotton white folios too delicate to touch let alone search manifest the conundra of function. Where does this book belong on the shelf? What's its utility, its purpose? Each folio its own room of the containing box's library. These rooms can be arranged and displayed as needed/desired but ultimately they belong to the library building as do the books they represent to libraries that house more information, more knowledge, more dreams, further condensation of the ephemeral stuff of breath: of sound, of tongues, of parchment, of airy white cotton soft as clouds you can't reach, of paper kissed with such delicate pressure that the words themselves disappear into the . . . from a distance I see whatever I want to see and arrange my ideas accordingly.

WHY NOT?

why not? he says
why not? she says
why not? they all say
they all say
i make things
i make things that have meaning
i make meaning
out of air
out of sight
out of mind
inward bent
in the space between
mind & brain
magic & particle
meaning & language
written or spoken
or imagined or unimagined

INTRODUCING THE SYNTHESIS

— About the Author —

Thy Synthesis was one composed from many. He wrote, "It's no wonder my conviction is steeped in contradiction. Take two fictions, put 'em together, and you got the prescription for something different: The Synthesis. Begin with this." His work was ongoing.